Anniversary Story Collection

60 Years of

Guide

Also by Lori Peckham:
Guide's Greatest Animal Stories
Guide's Greatest Change of Heart Stories
Guide's Greatest Grace Stories
Guide's Greatest Hero Stories
Guide's Greatest Mission Stories
Guide's Greatest Mystery Stories
Guide's Greatest Narrow Escape Stories
Guide's Greatest Rescue Stories
Insight Presents More Unforgettable Stories
Jesus in My Shoes

To order, call **1-800-765-6955**.
Visit us at **www.reviewandherald.com** for information on other Review and Herald® products.

A special thanks to the authors we were unable to locate. If anyone can provide knowledge of their current mailing address, please relay this information to Lori Peckham, in care of the Review and Herald® Publishing Association.

LORI PECKHAM, EDITOR

Anniversary
Story
Collection

60 Years of
Guide

REVIEW AND HERALD® PUBLISHING ASSOCIATION

Since 1861 | www.reviewandherald.com

Copyright © 2013 by Review and Herald® Publishing Association

Published by Review and Herald® Publishing Association, Hagerstown, MD 21741-1119

Review and Herald® titles may be purchased in bulk for educational, business, fund-raising, or sales promotional use. For information, please e-mail SpecialMarkets@reviewandherald.com.

The Review and Herald® Publishing Association publishes biblically based materials for spiritual, physical, and mental growth and Christian discipleship.

This book was
Edited by Lori Peckham
Interior designed by Tina M. Ivany
Cover designed by Mark Bond
Typeset: Minion 11/13

PRINTED IN U.S.A.

13 12 11 10 09   5 4 3 2 1

Library of Congress Cataloging-in-Publication Data

60 years of *Guide* : anniversary story collection / Lori Peckham, editor.

    pages cm

1. Christian life—Seventh-Day Adventists authors—Juvenile literature. 2. Christian education of children. 3. Seventh-Day Adventists—Customs and practices—Juvenile literature. I. Peckham, Lori. II. Robinson, Virgil E. Carried by a lion.
 BX6155.A15 2013
 242'.63—dc23

2013001493

ISBN 978-0-8280-2730-4

CONTENTS

Dedication and Thanks 8

A Note From the Current *Guide* Editor 9

Chapter 1: Carried by a Lion
Virgil Robinson / January 19, 1955 11

Chapter 2: So Easily Satisfied
Arthur S. Maxwell / November 30, 1955. 13

Chapter 3: "That Was My Back!"
Barbara Westphal / December 19, 1956 15

Chapter 4: Angel of the Crossing
Norma R. Youngberg / April 17, 1957 18

Chapter 5: The "Mystic Myths"
Enid Sparks / May 22, 1957 21

Chapter 6: Suicide Pilot
Lawrence Maxwell / January 21, 1959 24

Chapter 7: Mr. Roberts and the Noisy Horn Honker
Ivy R. Doherty / December 23, 1959 26

Chapter 8: B Is for Beer or Brains
D. Carl Anderson / May 31, 1961 30

Chapter 9: The Ghost in the Graveyard
Kay Heistand / October 16, 1963 32

Chapter 10: A Truckload of Victory
Josephine Cunnington Edwards / July 15, 1964 36

Chapter 11: Rashid's Broken Vow
Goldie Down / August 31, 1966 39

Chapter 12: Josie and the Hand-me-down
Dorothy Aitken / March 6, 1968 47

Chapter 13: When No One Pursues Them
Penny Estes Wheeler / May 5, 1971 50

Chapter 14: A Safe Play
Peggy Hodges / June 2, 1971 66

Chapter 15: For His Own Good
Lois Mae Cuhel / August 13, 1975 71

Chapter 16: Spring Training
Clare Miseles / May 12, 1976 75

Chapter 17: Sunshine Inside
Trudy J. Morgan / January 18, 1986 77

Chapter 18: The Fastest Bug
Jan S. Doward / July 26, 1986 81

Chapter 19: The Great Shoe Adventure
Mary Louise Kitsen / December 6, 1986 85

Chapter 20: The River
Maylan Schurch / August 26, 1989 88

Chapter 21: Fakebite
Randy Fishell / February 3, 1990 92

Chapter 22: Body Odor, Hairy Legs, and Stinkin' Skis
Karl Haffner / January 26, 1991 96

Chapter 23: Dangerous Dewey
Jack Calkins / July 27, 1991 100

Chapter 24: High-speed Hunt
Charles Mills / February 8, 1997 103

Chapter 25: My Nasty Victory
Jane Chase / January 31, 1998. 107

Chapter 26: Promises, Promises
Carolyn Rathbun / February 27, 1999. 110

Chapter 27: Jungle Fear
Helen Lee / March 11, 2000 114

Chapter 28: Pushing Through to Rawlins
Elaine Egbert / February 3, 2007 117

Chapter 29: Mystery Man on the Shore
Dawn Clark / March 24, 2007 120

Chapter 30: Janna's Offering
Elfriede Volk / December 18, 2010. 123

Dedicated to . . .

All the enthusiastic readers of these *Guide* story collections, especially my son, Reef, and his fifth- and sixth-grade classmates.

Special Thanks to . . .

The editors of *Guide* magazine over the years, all of whom I have had the privilege of meeting personally, and who have touched my life—and the lives of generations of young people.

Randy Fishell, the current editor of *Guide,* who, realizing the treasure of true stories buried in bound volumes of the magazine, initiated these story collections and continues to creatively direct them.

Tonya Ball, desktop technician, who makes the work of 60 years happen in a flash.

"You, O Lord, shall endure forever, and the remembrance of Your name to all generations" (Psalm 102:12, NKJV).

A Note From the Current Guide Editor

In his first editorial for *Junior Guide* Lawrence Maxwell wrote this about the new magazine: "It is our prayer that it will guide you all the way from earth to heaven."*

Sixty years later, this goal remains the same. Clothing and hairstyles change with each passing decade, but the power of a true story pointing to Jesus still moves hearts.

Yes, much has changed over the past six decades, but juniors and earliteens still need to know just how much God loves them. That's why we still work hard to provide glimpses of His grace through the pages of this little magazine called *Guide*.

As you enjoy the stories in this special sixtieth anniversary collection, maybe it will bring back warm memories of a time when you held the magazine in your hands as a young person. If you're a current junior or earliteen, this volume can serve as a kind of time machine, opening windows into bygone times.

Whatever kind of reader you happen to be, we wish you all of God's blessings as you enjoy this book. May His timeless story be written on your heart.

—Randy Fishell

Junior Guide, October 7, 1953, p. 2.

1

Carried by a Lion

by Virgil Robinson

The First World War was on, and troops from South Africa fought to take Southwest Africa from the Germans. Attached to the South African Army was a young man who acted as a scout. He carried with him a small portable radio, and night after night he would send in reports to headquarters. He had to live on cold foods out of tin cans, as he dared not make a fire. The smoke would give away his position. He also carried with him a light sleeping bag, which he carefully buttoned up every night. The days were warm, but the nights often got very cold.

As a sincere Christian, this young man never lay down to rest without a word of thanksgiving to his heavenly Father for keeping him safe through the day and a request that he might be protected through the night.

One morning, just as day began to dawn, he was awakened with the strangest sensation. He seemed to be moving somewhere. As he gradually came to, he opened his eyes and found that it was true. The ground was going by about a foot under his head. Something was carrying him. What could it be?

Slowly he turned his head around and up. His eyes rested upon the shaggy coat of an enormous lion. While he had been sleeping, this lion had passed by. Smelling a human being, it had investigated. With the greatest of ease the animal had picked up the young man in his sleeping bag—and so gently that the beast had not injured him in the least, nor even awakened him. Just where the lion was going with him the poor fellow had no idea, but it wasn't hard to guess!

The man could do nothing. He realized that if he shouted for help, or tried to get out of the sleeping bag, the lion would doubtless kill him with one blow of its paw. He could only hope and pray that God would cause something to happen to save him. And quickly! For surely the lion did not plan to carry him very far.

Fortunately, something did happen in time. Around the bend in the path came a party of local Africans out hunting. Seeing a strange bundle in the mouth of a lion, they shouted, hurling their spears at the wild animal. Disconcerted, the lion dropped the man and bounded away into the tall grass. The Africans opened the sleeping bag to let the young man out, for at the last moment he had fainted from fright. He soon recovered and ever after told how God had saved him from the lion.

2
So Easily Satisfied
by Arthur S. Maxwell

It was just two weeks before Christmas, and everybody was talking about Christmas presents.

So were John and Charlie. Both boys wondered what they would find in their stockings on the great and happy morning.

When Daddy called them into his study one evening, they both thought he might—well, he just might—want to talk to them about Christmas presents.

And for once they were right.

As John seated himself on Daddy's right knee and Charlie on Daddy's left knee, Daddy said, "Well, boys, I thought I would ask you what you would like for Christmas."

"Goody! Goody!" they gurgled with delight.

At this moment Daddy noticed that John had brought a book with him. A big, fat book.

"What do you have there?" asked Daddy.

"A catalog."

"A what?" said Daddy, a big smile breaking out on his face.

"A catalog. You know, from the department store."

"Oh, I see!" said Daddy. "I was wondering."

"It's very interesting," said John.

"Oh, I am sure," said Daddy. "John, seeing you are the older, you shall be first. Now tell me, what would you like most for Christmas?"

John didn't answer at once. Instead he opened his book and pointed to something on page one. "I think I'd like that," he said.

Then he turned over the page and pointed to something on page 2. "I think I'd like this," he said.

Then he turned to page 3, and page 4, and page 5, and so on, all through the book. On almost every page he saw something he thought he wanted. It looked as though he must have been studying the catalog for a long time.

When he reached the last page, he closed the book with a sigh. It had taken him exactly a half hour to go through it. His wants included a bicycle, a boat, a canoe, a fishing rod, a penknife, a flashlight, an airplane, a helicopter, a pair of skates, all sorts of games, and I don't know what else.

"Is that all?" asked Daddy.

"I think so," said John. "For the time being, anyway."

Daddy laughed out loud. Then he turned to Charlie. "Well, Charlie, now it's your turn. What would you like for Christmas?"

Charlie was only 5 years old, two years younger than his big brother, John. He wasn't old enough yet to read catalogs.

Looking up into Daddy's face with a sweet, innocent smile, he said, "Daddy, anything will do for me. You see, I'm so easily satisfied."

Tears came into Daddy's eyes as he drew Charlie very close. "You dear, dear boy!" he exclaimed.

And John told me—for John is all grown up now—that from that moment on he was sure Daddy loved Charlie more than he loved him. I don't know about that, but it certainly was a very beautiful thing that Charlie said.

There are lots of Johns and lots of Charlies in the world. In other words, there are lots of boys and girls who seem to be carrying catalogs around with them, always wanting this and that and the other thing—rather selfishly, I'm afraid. And there are lots of the other kind, too—the gentle, caring, unselfish boys and girls who are so easily satisfied, so glad for anything that Mother or Daddy may give them.

I have even met some "Johns" who look upon the Bible as a sort of catalog. They search and search through it for all the beautiful things they hope to have in God's wonderland of tomorrow. You know—the golden streets and pearly gates; the tree of life with its glorious fruit; the river of life with its refreshing water; a mansion in the city and another in the country. They think that all these things will keep them happy forever and ever.

But the "Charlies" are different. They say, with King David of old, "Because I have lived right, I will see your face. When I wake up, I will see your likeness and be satisfied" (Psalm 17:15, NCV).

Just to be like Jesus, just to see Him face to face . . . that is all they ask.

So easily satisfied! Yes, and so wonderfully satisfied!

Somehow I think it will be these—the boys and girls with Charlie's sweet, unselfish spirit—whom God will want closest to Him in His kingdom. For they will be happy, contented, and satisfied forever, just to be with Him.

3
"That Was My Back!"
by Barbara Westphal

One moonlit night Julian and his two friends were walking home from an evening meeting. They were lay preachers in Mexico. Although they didn't receive any pay for their missionary work, they gave all their spare time to preaching.

They felt especially happy that particular night because nearly 75 people had attended the meeting, and eight of them had accepted Christ as their Savior.

The path to their village was very narrow, and they were walking one in front of the other. Beside the trail they noticed several men waiting for them. The moonlight shone on long knives called machetes in their belts.

"Who are you? What are you doing in this lonely place so late at night?" one of the armed men demanded angrily.

"I am Julian, and my companions and I have been preaching in the village back there. Jesus is coming soon, and we want the people to get ready," Julian explained.

A curse was the only answer Julian and his friends heard.

They began to pass by the rough men, praying in their hearts (without shutting their eyes) that the Lord would protect them from those gleaming machetes.

The first preacher passed safely. Then the second one got by. But as Julian came along, the first two heard a terrible blow. Quickly they looked back, guessing that Julian had been hit by one of the men with a machete. But Julian was walking along as if nothing had happened.

As soon as they got safely beyond hearing, one of them said, "What a blow that man gave the ground with his machete!"

"The ground, nothing!" exclaimed Julian. "That was my back!"

His friends rushed to him and lifted up his loose white shirt to see his wound. But they couldn't see even a mark.

"Didn't you feel it?" they asked.

"Yes, but it seemed like just a gentle tap, as if a child had touched me," he replied.

"A miracle!" they repeated softly, and three thank-You prayers went up to God for taking care of Julian.

The next morning the man who had hit Julian woke up feeling sick. As the hours passed he grew rapidly worse. There was no doctor in his village, nor in any nearby village.

"In the village of Zaragoza there is a young man named Julian who could give you some medicine and help you," a friend told him.

"Julian!" the sick man cried. "Why, I gave him such a cut with my machete last night that he must be dead by now!"

"Julian dead? Oh, no, you're wrong. I saw him myself this morning when I went to the market in Zaragoza. There's nothing the matter with him."

The fever rose higher and the pains became so severe that the poor man thought surely he would die. The next morning his friends took him to Zaragoza.

When they asked people in the village who could treat him, everyone responded, "A young man named Julian would be the best one to help you. God is with him, and the people he takes care of get well."

When Julian heard that his enemy wanted to see him, do you suppose he said, "What? That man who tried to strike me down with a machete? Just let him suffer. That's what he deserves!"? No. Julian called some friends in and said, "Remember I told you that last night a rough fellow gave me a blow with a machete? Well, he is sick and has sent for me. Pray that I'll know how to help him and that God will touch his heart."

While they prayed, Julian took care of his enemy, giving him some simple treatments and remedies. When the sick man felt better, he was ashamed of himself and asked Julian to forgive him.

"Ask God to forgive you, not me," replied the lay preacher. "I was just obeying God's commands when I went to have that meeting in your village. And besides," he added, "the machete didn't hurt me. My God took care of me. You just hit me with the broad side of the machete anyway, and God didn't let me feel it."

Machetes have both a broad side and a sharp edge. It's bad enough to be hit with the flat side of the blade, but it's much worse to be cut with the edge.

"But I hit you with the sharp edge," the sick man confessed. "And I hit so hard that I thought I would kill you."

The man—who was soon as good as new—became Julian's friend, and everyone in the villages heard that the Adventist lay preacher had made his enemy well, with Jesus' help. After that, when Julian went to have meetings in nearby villages, there was no one throwing stones, or making fun, or waiting on a dark trail with machetes. Instead, the people waited expectantly for the three lay preachers to come and tell them about Jesus.

4
Angel of the Crossing
by Norma R. Youngberg

The little South Dakota city lay smothered in deep white drifts. Along the streets workers shoveled and dug to clear the roads, but the streetcars had not run for days.

"I don't think the elder should try to go out on a night like this," Aunt Nellie said to Uncle Hale. "You know he doesn't see as well as he used to."

They looked out into the night. The snow lay several feet high along the sides of the street. A high wind whistled around the corners of the house.

Uncle Hale went to the door of the front bedroom and called, "Elder Goodman, you'd better skip that Bible study tonight. It's windy and cold. If it starts snowing again, there will be a real blizzard."

Elder Goodman emerged from the bedroom dressed for going out, with his fur cap and heavy overcoat. He held the little satchel with the books and charts he needed for giving the Bible study.

Just then Jackie, who was 12, walked into the room. His family lived on a farm in the country, and he came into town and stayed with Aunt Nellie and Uncle Hale during the winter so he could attend school.

"It does look bad, doesn't it?" the elder remarked, glancing out the window. "I wouldn't go if that woman wasn't so sick. You see, she might get worse and die, and this series of Bible studies may be the last chance she will have to learn about God."

He pulled down the fur-lined tabs of his cap and wrapped his muffler snuggly about his throat. "I promised the family I'd surely come tonight, and they'll be expecting me. I'd hate to disappoint them."

"Let me go with Elder Goodman," Jackie spoke up. "I went to school today, and it isn't much worse now than it was then."

"It's too bad for either of you to venture out." Aunt Nellie shook her head. "But if the good elder is set on going, I'd feel better if you went with him."

Jackie hurried upstairs, and within five minutes he was back, dressed for the walk. He wore a fur cap, a sheepskin jacket, thick trousers, and heavy leggings and overshoes. The two stepped out into the night and started to walk the eight blocks that lay between their home and the place where Elder Goodman planned to give the study.

They reached the east side of town beyond the railroad tracks, close to the packinghouse district. It was necessary to cross a spur of the railroad that ran to one of the big packing sheds. This spur was seldom used, and there was no marker except the wooden cross usually displayed at railway crossings. Both Elder Goodman and Jackie crossed this place every day, and neither of them had ever seen a train there. In fact, tonight they forgot that the rails lay under the snow. They weren't thinking of trains or railroads at all, but were talking about the snow. Elder Goodman loved to come up with object lessons whenever he had the chance.

"Do you know, Jackie," he said now, "that in all these drifts of snow there are no two flakes exactly the same?"

"You mean they're all different? Aren't there ever two alike?"

"I suppose there have never been two people born into this world who were exactly alike, and no two flakes of snow have been just alike either," Elder Goodman explained.

Jackie thought about this for several minutes. The cold snow crunched under their feet. Here and there a star shone between the dark clouds that scudded across the sky.

Elder Goodman spoke again. "If God cares enough for the snowflakes that He takes special care to make each one different, what do you think of His care for us?"

"I guess we should recognize that God knows all about us and loves us." Jackie pulled his muffler tighter around his throat. "I don't think He needed to make all the snowflakes different. He could have made a few hundred kinds. That would surely have shown how great and good He is."

"You remember that God has counted all the hairs on our head. He needn't have bothered about that either, but He did. And it shows us how much He is interested in every one of us and how much wiser and more careful He is than any human being."

The wind grew worse every minute. It was no longer possible to talk. The screaming blast caught away their words, and both of the travelers wrapped their coats closer about them and walked on, leaning into the wind. It was now only two blocks more to the house where they would give the study.

Then the snow began to fall—large flakes driven by the icy wind, till they stung like hot cinders. Elder Goodman walked ahead, with Jackie close behind him. The streetlamps were bright here, and they could see the way.

Then suddenly Elder Goodman stumbled backward several steps, almost knocking Jackie over. And out of the night came a thunderous roar and a blinding light. An engine whizzed past so close that they could have reached out and touched it!

"It was an angel!" the older man exclaimed.

Jackie heard him, but his voice was caught away by the shrieking wind. A few minutes later in the home where they had come to give the Bible study, Elder Goodman told what had happened.

"I was bent forward into the wind, with all my attention fixed on keeping straight ahead through the blinding snow. Jackie was following me. I saw nothing and heard nothing but the fierce wind. Then suddenly a hand was laid on my chest. It was as though a giant had laid his great hand against me and pushed me. I ran backward several steps just as the engine roared past."

"It must have been one of God's angels at the crossing," Jackie spoke up. "He was sent to take care of us."

That night the Bible study was most tenderly given and gladly received. Faith entered into the sick woman, and she began to get better. And the angel of the crossing surely had a smile on his face and satisfaction in his heart.

5
The "Mystic Myths"
by Enid Sparks

Hazel came home from school as gloomy as a three-day rain. But when Mother tried to find out what the trouble was, she would only say, "Oh, nothing much!" She wearily placed her schoolbooks on the dining table.

"But there is something wrong," insisted Mother. "Come and tell me about it and you'll feel better." Mother moved over on the sofa, and Hazel sat down beside her.

"Jill never invited me to her party. I hate to be snubbed all the time. I guess she thought I wouldn't have a new dress to wear," blurted Hazel, tossing the hair from her face and wiping away a tear from her cheek.

"Oh, just clothes trouble." Mother smiled, looking kindly at the dejected expression on Hazel's face. "How many heartaches such little things can cause."

"Not a very little thing if you ask me," sighed Hazel.

"I can tell you how to be happy if you're willing to try," said Mother.

"How?" Hazel grunted.

"To be happy," continued Mother, "make someone else happy. Who are some of the other girls that Jill and her clique have nothing to do with? Can't you girls get together and form a club to make others happy? Maybe someday you could even help Jill!"

"Oh, Mom, don't be funny. Who could ever help Jill? When would she need any help? She has so many pretty dresses and such beautiful wavy hair," Hazel said.

"I'm serious," answered Mother. "Just try my scheme for a few days."

"Well, all right," said Hazel. "I sure hope it works."

She began to think out loud. "There's Janie, whose clothes always look threadbare. The girls call Judy 'carrottop' because of her red hair and many freckles. Then there's Ruth, the new girl. And Trudie is only 10; Jill thinks she's too young for their group."

"You five girls could form a secret club," added Mother. "Maybe you'd like to give it a name, and when you do something, you could leave a little note signed with your secret name. I think you'd have a lot of fun keeping it all a mystery."

"Oh, that sounds good!" Hazel laughed. "But what could we call ourselves? The Kindness Club? No. The Misfit Misses? No. I don't like that, either." Then she let out a shout. "I know! The Mystic Myths. That's what we'll be. Wait till I tell the girls tomorrow!"

The girls liked the idea as soon as she told them, and in no time at all they had their club organized.

When Grandmother Brown went to town and returned, she found her apples all picked off the ground and put in boxes by her cellar door, with a piece of paper on top saying, "Mystic Myths."

"Who are they?" she asked in wonder. But there was no other clue. "Well, they must be mighty nice, whoever they are," she decided.

Each girl found something to do to help someone else. Trudie took care of Mrs. Neil's baby when she had to go on an errand. Hazel and Judy took turns helping Mrs. Smith with her ironing. Ruth persuaded her brother to help her stack Mrs. Nichol's load of blocks. Whenever possible, they kept their deeds a secret.

One day as Hazel was coming in from the playground she passed Jill on the steps and noticed that she had been crying. Hazel leaned over to ask her whether she could help in any way.

"Oh, no one likes me anymore," sobbed Jill.

"Yes, they do," comforted Hazel.

"No, they don't—I know they don't." And Jill swished away before Hazel could say another word.

The Mystic Myths met in special session that afternoon as soon as school let out. They decided they would give Jill a box of the cookies they had made when they had had their latest club meeting at Hazel's house. Janie found a pretty card and wrote on it "From the Mystic Myths, your friends." The next day Ruth put the box on Jill's desk.

Jill uttered an exclamation of surprise when she saw it. But when she opened it and found the cookies inside, she squeaked, "I know they're no good. Someone wants to make me sick."

Judy was standing nearby and said, "I'm sure they must be all right. I'll eat one to prove to you that they aren't poison."

"Oh," gasped Jill, "you must know something about them. Do you know who the Mystic Myths are? Daisy and Sue and I have been trying so hard to find out. So many people have found little notes signed just 'Mystic Myths.' They are so clever."

"How would you like to join our club?" Hazel invited. "We have a motto: 'To be happy, help someone.'"

"Well, it's awfully nice of you girls to ask me after the way I've treated you. I'd love to join, and I'm sure Daisy and Sue would, too."

So that afternoon the mystery went out of the Mystic Myths. But it was all right. Everyone was friends at last.

6

Suicide Pilot

by Lawrence Maxwell

The following pilots are ordered to crash their planes directly into the side of an American bomber. Shomiko, Sakae . . ."

The voice went on, but Sakae paid no attention to it. He grinned. This was the day he had been waiting for. Today he would die for the emperor—and the crew of an American bomber would die with him.

All the 20 years of his life he had been living for today. All his life he had been taught to hate his enemies. At 14 he left home to attend a military school. Later he trained as a pilot and became an officer in the Japanese air force.

The year he was 16, Japanese bombers attacked Pearl Harbor and Japan was at war. Soon enemy bombers began attacking Japanese cities.

Sakae was ordered into the air to fight off these attacks. Vigorously he fired on the bombers, and as vigorously the bombers fired back. But Sakae always returned to his home base safely.

The bombing attacks became more frequent. New methods would have to be worked out to stop them. The Japanese government asked the fighter pilots if some of them would be willing to crash their planes right into the American bombers.

Sakae volunteered. If he crashed against an enemy bomber, he would be sure to die for the emperor.

After that, when there was an enemy attack, several of the pilots would be told they were to crash into the bombers. These men never came back.

Sakae waited impatiently to hear his name read, but weeks passed, and always it was other pilots who were ordered to fly the suicide planes.

Then it came. August 14, 1945. Sirens wailed. B-29s were attacking! Action stations! And a voice over the loudspeaker: "The following pilots are ordered to crash their planes directly into the side of an American bomber. Shomiko, Sakae . . ."

Sakae grinned. Today he would roar into the blue above and die for the emperor. He ran for his plane and climbed aboard. The engine roared. A man at the far end of the runway prepared to signal him off.

But now another man was running across the landing field, waving frantically. "The war is over!" he shouted. "Japan has surrendered."

Disgusted, Sakae switched off the engine and walked wearily to his quarters. The war was over. Now he wouldn't get a chance to kill his enemy. Now he couldn't die for the emperor.

Hard times followed for Sakae. When he got home, he found his house burned and his mother and other relatives dead.

Then one evening, as he was feeling lonely, he saw a pretty girl reading a book. He wanted to talk to her, so he decided to ask about the book.

She said it was a Bible, but he didn't know what that was. She said it had been sent to Japan by the American Bible Society.

"It's American!" he scoffed. "I'll have nothing to do with it—or you!"

But he decided he did want to have more to do with the girl. She liked the Bible, so he let her talk about it as much as she wanted to.

The more he heard, the more *he* liked. And one day the young man who used to think that big, noisy airplanes were the most important things in life found that a little, silent Book was more important than anything else.

He accepted the God of his enemy. He decided to live for the Emperor of heaven, King Jesus. He went to a religious college, graduated, and then married the girl. Later he became pastor of a church near Tokyo.

Strange how God works out His plans in people's lives, isn't it? Are you letting Him work out His plans in your life?

7
Mr. Roberts and the Noisy Horn Honker
by Ivy R. Doherty

Snowflakes as big as powder puffs fell from the sky. Mr. Roberts could see almost nothing as his car crawled along in the deep rut that had been made by other cars. A brisk wind shrieked around the vehicle, and Beverly snuggled closer to her father. She couldn't help wondering what they would do if the drifts became so deep that they couldn't get home.

Home and Mother were still about 10 miles away, and the snowstorm was by no means over.

The crunch of the snow as it groaned under the wheels and the clickety-click of the tire chains were the only sounds that broke the monotony. That is, they were the only sounds until a sleek black car came closer from behind. The driver honked his horn. Apparently he was in a big hurry and had no patience for anyone in his way.

"For pity's sake!" Mr. Roberts muttered. "Just how does that fellow expect me to let him pass? He's in my rut. He'll have to stay behind me. If I should move a half foot, I'd be bogged down to the doors in snow."

Beverly did not comment. She knew how little her father liked her to make suggestions when he was driving. Perhaps if the man in the black car knew how her father hated being honked at, he'd think a little more seriously before he dared touch the horn again.

But no, the man in the black car had no notion of letting the horn rest. He honked every time he felt like honking, which was very frequently indeed. Mr. Roberts controlled his temper pretty well for three long, slow miles. He was just about to burst into fury when, fortunately, the rut spread out and made a kind of detour. Beverly's heart leaped with gladness, for her father pulled over a bit and let the black car pass.

One more honk, and the black car disappeared into the falling snow ahead.

"Thanks be for that!" sighed Mr. Roberts. "Now we can jog along in our own rut, at our own pace. What a bothersome fellow he was. I hope he gets stuck. It would serve him right for being so impatient. Yes, I do hope he gets stuck!"

Beverly said nothing. There was nothing to say. She hoped that her father didn't really mean what he had said and that he would be sorry as soon as he "cooled off." It would be pretty uncomfortable being bogged down in a snowdrift.

The *scrape, scrape* of the windshield wipers lulled Beverly's sleepy eyes. So did the warmth from the heater. The girl must have dozed, for her father's voice was startlingly loud when he said, "I never saw the like!"

She scrambled up from where she had been leaning against his shoulder to see what it was that her father had never seen before. Oh, it was the black car! It had plowed deep into the snow. And as Father drove closer Beverly could see the horn honker digging furiously into a drift, trying to get the black car out.

"He at least had the sense to bring a shovel," Mr. Roberts remarked, putting his foot down harder on the gas. If he felt any compassion for the dejected digger in the snow, it was soon wiped out by the irritating memory of the way the man had honked his horn so much.

Beverly wasn't cold, but she shivered as she snuggled close to her father again. Perhaps she was shivering out of sympathy for the stranded man. She wished in her heart that her father hadn't passed him by so hastily. What if she were sitting in that car waiting for her father to dig them out? What if they had seen someone go by without offering to help? She shuddered.

Ah! There was the sign that pointed down the road toward home! They were just five miles from Mother, a good meal, and a crackling fire in the living room.

No more than two cars had turned off the highway onto this road all day. That was plain to see. There was a little rut, but the snow had fallen steadily, and now the rut was scarcely visible.

Mr. Roberts had great faith in his tire chains, but they were not enough protection. The car went into a slow slide, swung around, and plunged off the road. It settled solidly and obstinately in deep snow.

Beverly said nothing. There was again nothing for her to say. Mr. Roberts was also grimly silent. He had many things to think about— especially his remark regarding the shovel that the horn-honking man had thoughtfully put in the trunk of his car. He thought about how he had laughed at that driver. He had felt a suspicion all along that he had been too hard-hearted and far too irritable, but up until now he had managed not to let the feeling bother him very much. Now he could see everything in a different light. He could see that he was a selfish man.

"We'll either have to walk or wait for someone to come along," he told Beverly. "I think we ought to wait on the chance that someone will come by soon."

The minutes ticked along, leadenly. Every one of them seemed like an hour. The wind howled like a pack of coyotes—hungry coyotes. The snow flew around like a swarm of white bees. Every living thing seemed to have disappeared. *This car could as well be in Greenland or even in Antarctica,* Beverly thought, *but the sign at the crossroads says home is only five miles away.*

A half hour crawled by. Mr. Roberts said, "Beverly, I'm afraid we'll have to walk home. I know it is not wise in this blizzard, but neither is it wise to stay in the car. To remain here with evening coming on would be suicide."

Beverly reluctantly crept from the car and stretched her stiff legs. The wind seemed to cut through her. It felt doubly cold because she had sat so long in the heated automobile.

A soft purring sound came to her through the wailing of the wind. Could it be, oh, could it be? The sound died under the roar of the blizzard. She shivered again and strained her ears, hoping desperately to hear that purring sound once more. She took the strong hand her father offered and plunged ahead with him into the snow. It was truly a journey of a step at a time.

For Beverly the going was worse than for Mr. Roberts, for her legs were much shorter than his. Each time her foot sank deep in the snow she despaired of its ever coming back up again. At the rate they were progressing there was no possible hope of reaching home before nightfall. With every step Beverly breathed a prayer, asking God to care for them in their need.

They had traveled no more than a few yards when the unmistakable sound of an engine reached them. A car drove up the hill to the crossroads, hesitated long enough for the driver to read the signs, then sped on its way. Mr. Roberts' cry for help faded away in the blizzard. "Perhaps we are doing the wrong thing," he said. "You go back and sit in the car for a while. I will stand at the signpost and wait for the next car."

It was wonderful relief for Beverly to be back within shelter. But for Mr. Roberts it was a long wait for the next car. He paced back and forth, back and forth, trying to keep warm. His feet and hands ached cruelly. His body shivered in spite of himself. He was just about ready to give way to despair when he heard the most wonderful music—the throb of another engine.

Mr. Roberts and the Noisy Horn Honker

Over the incline came . . . a sleek black car! At the wheel was no other person than the honking driver.

How the tables had turned! Mr. Roberts felt sure that the man would recognize him and his bogged car and pass on his way. He knew that he deserved no better treatment after the mean spirit he had shown.

He was about to turn back to his car when the horn honked and the driver got out. "In very deep?" he asked, opening his trunk and taking out the trusty shovel. "We'll get you back on the road in just a little while."

Beverly could hardly believe her eyes when she saw who their rescuer was. *That's how it is,* she thought. *Sometimes a person harbors meanness in his soul and he is suddenly made terribly ashamed by the very person he treated badly.*

Mr. Roberts and Mr. Cobham (for that was the car honker's name) took turns digging the snow and tramping a place solid enough for the car to swerve back into the only rut on the road toward home.

There was something about the cheerful, purposeful way Mr. Cobham worked that Beverly would never forget. When the job was done, he slapped Mr. Roberts' back in a friendly way and said, "Well, old fellow, stick to your rut, and a safe journey. This is one time in your life when it is good to be in a rut!"

He opened Beverly's door an inch or two and said, "Take care of yourself and your father, young lady." He gave her a big wink and turned back to his car.

Mr. Roberts was very quiet for the remainder of the tedious journey. It took all his powers of concentration to stay in the rut. Beverly's brothers, Tommy and Billy, had cleared the way from the road to the garage so that the car was able to leave the rut safely. Home had never looked so good.

As the family sat around the table eating Mother's delicious dinner, Mr. Roberts recounted the events of the trip home. Then he said, "Some of us go a long way through life before we completely learn how to live the golden rule. I had the best lesson today I've ever had on the subject. I want my children to learn that same lesson while they are still young. Then they will make the world a better place to live in."

Warmth glowed in Beverly's heart. She loved her father. He was a good man, for only a good man would recognize his mistake and confess it so that his children would learn to be better people. She suddenly felt a great desire always to be kind, and right then she promised God that she would live to make the world a better place for everyone.

8
B Is for Beer or Brains
by D. Carl Anderson

"A nd now," the loudspeaker blared out, "as the final act of this air show, Tim Johnson will fly to 5,000 feet, bail out, and fall for 3,000 feet before opening his parachute."

"Wow!" I exclaimed. "How does he do it?"

"Well," said Dad, "it takes skill and quick thinking, but these men have a lot of experience and good coordination."

Tim had all of these, I reasoned. He had made several jumps today already and was really good. I hurried over toward the hangar and waited.

Then suddenly a sight met my eyes that I'll never forget. Tim Johnson had a can of beer in his hand! He was foolishly jesting with everyone, afraid of nothing. As I saw him drinking, I worried, for I knew that alcohol numbs the brain and slows down a person's reaction time.

But soon Tim was on his way. He walked right beside me, still clutching his can of beer. He climbed with it into his plane and then threw it—empty—to the ground. His plane rapidly gained altitude, but I couldn't help wondering if he knew what he was doing to himself.

The plane wound higher and higher to 2,000, 3,000, 4,000 feet. Slowly the alcohol was taking effect, and Tim was growing braver. He announced that he would go to 8,000 feet and drop to 2,000 feet before opening his parachute. Cheers and clapping arose from the crowd, and the plane circled higher. With each circle, Tim felt braver, and finally he announced that he would go to 10,000 feet, bail out, and drop to 1,000 feet before opening his chute.

Oohs and aahs of amazement went out from the crowd.

"How can he do it?" someone asked.

"He's really terrific!" said another.

As the plane made its final round, I saw a tiny speck fall away from it. Faster and faster it came. Now we could see it was a man.

The audience was deathly silent as Tim came closer . . . closer. He kept gaining speed, and still his parachute did not open.

"Why doesn't he open it?" cried a voice.

"He'll be killed!" shrieked another.

"Please, open it!" a woman pleaded.

There were many silent and audible prayers, but still Tim sped nearer, nearer, nearer. Then suddenly the chute started to blossom, there was a cloud of dust . . . and life was all over for Tim.

People screamed and cried. Many of them started running toward the spot where Tim's body had hit the ground, and the rest of the people sadly turned toward home.

I'll always picture in my mind the scene of Tim Johnson holding the can of beer that cost him his life. If his reaction time had been the slightest bit faster, he would have pulled his parachute cord sooner and would have landed safely.

Tim made his choice. He chose beer instead of life. What will your choice be?

9
The Ghost in the Graveyard
by Kay Heistand

"It was a ghost! I tell you, I saw it with my own eyes!" The voice speaking was very excited.

Denny looked at his brother, his blue eyes opening wide. He began to say something, but Gene quickly laid a finger across his lips so he couldn't.

Both boys were squatting on the grass near the front porch, hidden from sight by the thick foliage of the syringa bushes. Their father sat on the porch swing, reading the evening paper. Bo Stillman was talking to him.

Bo Stillman was high-strung all the time. But the boys noticed that he was even more nervous than usual tonight. And when they heard Bo say he had seen a ghost—seen it with his own eyes—they had to hear more!

"Now, Bo, take it easy." Father's voice was calm. "Slow down and tell me the whole story."

Bo's voice rose louder as he insisted, "I was taking a shortcut to town, so I decided to go through the old graveyard."

"I'm surprised you'd do that." The boys could tell by the sound of Father's voice that he was grinning. "After all, the cemetery is in that thickly wooded hollow. Remember how many times we were scared when we were boys?" Father chuckled.

Bo grunted. "Of course I remembered, especially after I'd gotten started through the graveyard, so I just pulled my coat collar up around my ears and wasted no time! But all at once I heard this rattling noise near a headstone. When I looked in that direction—it was by that Talbot monument—guess what I saw?"

"Moonlight!" Father scoffed.

Denny grabbed his brother's arm tight. Gene grinned, wrinkling his freckled nose.

"Nope, 'twarn't moonlight. There was something there—a white shape bobbing up and down close to that there headstone, and making a crackling noise, too. I took off outta there at 60 miles an hour!"

"Oh, come now, Bo." Father laughed. "It's sure funny how a little wind and moonlight can scare a grown man!"

"Seems to me somebody oughta investigate that old graveyard just the same," Bo said stubbornly. "I've heard that other folks have seen a ghost there too."

"Lemonade, anyone?"

The boys heard their mother come out on the porch, evidently carrying a pitcher of lemonade, and all discussion of ghosts stopped abruptly. Gene and Denny crawled out from under the syringa bushes and headed for the lemonade pitcher.

Denny forgot the talk about ghosts as he munched Mother's warm gingerbread and drank two glasses of lemonade. But as soon as he was in bed that night and the lights were out, he began remembering. He tossed and turned in his bunk bed, trying to find a comfortable spot.

"Denny?"

Denny jumped at the sound of his brother's voice, but he answered, "Aren't you asleep?"

"Of course I'm not! Would I be talking to you if I were? You know," Gene muttered, "Bo's right."

"Right about what?" Denny asked.

"About investigating that old graveyard." Gene spoke firmly.

"You're nuts!" Denny grunted. "Not me! I wouldn't go near the place!" He pulled the covers up about his shoulders.

"You're afraid," Gene jeered.

Denny didn't answer. He knew he was afraid, but he hated to admit it to his brother. Gene was older and bigger and never seemed scared.

"Aw, Denny, there's no such thing as ghosts," Gene said reassuringly.

"Uh-huh," Denny mumbled.

Suddenly Gene sat up, swung his legs around, and got out of bed.

Denny stared at his brother's shadow in the moonlight. "What are you doing?" he squeaked.

"I'm going to the graveyard." Excitement tinged Gene's voice, and he laughed softly as he reached for his jeans. "C'mon, Den. Are you going to let me go alone?"

Denny couldn't speak for a moment, but he finally forced out the words, "All right. But I think you're crazy. Mom and Dad won't like this a bit."

"Don't use them for an excuse." Gene pulled a sweater over his head and groped in his desk for something.

Denny grumbled as he dressed. *It seems like I'm always following Gene into something,* he thought.

33

Gene had found his flashlight and was testing it. "Works fine," he said. "C'mon, Denny!"

The boys crept downstairs, carefully avoiding the third step from the bottom. It always creaked.

Outside they found a typical October night—cool and crisp, with a smell in the air of burned leaves and advancing winter. Denny shivered a little under his sweater.

The boys struck out of town toward the old cemetery. In the small Ohio town where they lived they knew each road so well that the darkness made little difference to them. They had often been to the old graveyard, but never before at night!

The moon played hide-and-seek behind the clouds, and Gene used the flashlight sparingly. No one else seemed to be out.

When they reached the graveyard, Gene stopped a moment. He whispered to Denny, "Wasn't it by the old Talbot headstone where Bo saw the ghost?"

"I-I think so," Denny stammered. "Don't you think we ought to go home, Gene?"

"Of course not!" Gene exclaimed. "We've come this far; we can't back down now."

Gene led the way cautiously toward the large white tombstone that marked the final resting place of the Talbot family. Now the moon was so bright that he didn't have to use the flashlight at all. Denny noticed, however, that for all the brave words Gene used, he still looked around quickly and uneasily. Even his freckles appeared paler!

A few yards from the Talbot headstone Gene stopped and signaled Denny to do likewise.

The boys crouched behind another headstone and watched. Denny had to grit his teeth to keep them from chattering, and he was afraid he'd begin shivering again. He kept hoping they wouldn't see anything and could start toward home soon.

Then he heard a dry rattle in the bushes on the other side of the Talbot headstone. The rattling grew louder, and Denny grabbed Gene's arm.

Gene's whole body was tense. His eyes never left the spot from which the noise came.

Something white appeared in the bushes and began bobbing up and down. Through his fright Denny saw Gene drop the flashlight, and he knew suddenly that his brother was as frightened as he was.

Then they heard a muffled moan. Denny shut his eyes tightly in terror.

He heard the dry rattle again, and he knew the ghost was still there—white and eerie above the Talbot tombstone.

The muffled moan sounded again, and to his astonishment Denny heard his brother laugh. Then Gene was shaking him as he cried, "Look, Denny, look! And what does that moan sound like?"

Denny couldn't tell for the life of him.

"It's a cow!" Gene shouted. He dropped Denny's arm and advanced bravely toward the "ghost." He picked up the flashlight and turned it full on the apparition. The beam of light revealed the surprised face of an old white-faced cow!

"Look here, Denny, she's learned a new trick!" Gene exclaimed. "She found out if she stuck her head through these dry branches of this big lilac bush and bobbed her head up and down, she could scratch both sides of her neck at the same time."

Gene patted the cow and then bent over with laughter. "Oh, ho, ho! Wait till I tell Bo about this!"

Denny laughed too, but he thought, *I'd never have dared to come here if it hadn't been for Gene.*

Then something else struck him. *I'll bet most of the fears I have are imaginary ones, and if I'd just go ahead and face what I'm afraid of, it probably wouldn't turn out to be any worse than this old cow that everybody thought was a ghost!*

This important conclusion stayed with Denny. Throughout the years many anticipated fears and troubles proved not nearly so bad as he had thought, once he had faced up to them. No, Denny was never to forget the "ghost in the graveyard" or the lesson an old black cow with a white face taught him.

10
A Truckload of Victory

by Josephine Cunnington Edwards

"I can't buy anything fancy, nor any knickknacks," Mother told the children. "Don't ask me to, for I must save the money until Daddy is well again."

Mike's heart sank. His birthday was coming soon. But his father had been ill, and a great deal of money had been spent for the doctor.

"Surely they will get me a birthday present!" Mike said to himself. "Mother won't miss my birthday!"

Mike had two things wrong with him, both of which were very ugly. One was that he was selfish and always wanted the best for himself. He was conquering this selfishness a little at a time, with the help of Father and Mother.

But there was a more terrible enemy Mike needed to conquer—his temper. He would get so angry that he would grit his teeth, shut his eyes, and scream one furious thing after another. Father talked to him. Sometimes he took things away from him; and once he gave him a sound whipping. It helped a little, but Mike was still not a conqueror.

Mother talked to him, Auntie did, and Grandpa often said he'd come to some bad end if he did not get the best of his angry ways.

He tried—once in a while. He prayed sometimes—a little. But he did not really get down in earnest about it.

In the hardware store Mike had spotted a red dump truck trimmed in chrome, and he had wanted it for a long time. Father told him once, before he got sick, that Mike could have it if he would conquer his two bad enemies.

So Mike began watching himself carefully. "You pick out my piece of cake, Mother," he would say, or "You tell me when I ought to let Tom play with my new ball."

Now his birthday was coming up, and Father was sick again. Would he get the truck?

Mike got up at the break of day on his birthday. He hurried and cleaned his room and then went out and swept the porches. He wanted to be extra-good on his birthday and start the year right.

Father got up too. "I think I'll be able to go to work Monday," he told Mother, smiling. Then Mike came in with the broom.

"Happy birthday, son!" he said, patting Mike's shoulder. "If you've got your work done, you might go look on the dining room table. There's something there for a boy who has been a pretty good conqueror lately."

Mike managed to gasp out, "Thank you, Father." Then he fell over a rug and knocked down a chair in his haste to get to the dining room.

There on the table sat a great oblong package tied securely with brown string. Mike took time to untie it carefully, for it was a fine piece of cord and he knew his mother would want to keep it. Would his truck be inside?

It was! The beautiful dump truck he had feasted his eyes on for so long! Mother and Father smiled at him from the doorway. He went and kissed them both and thanked them.

For two weeks Mike had great fun with that dump truck. No one dreamed that down inside of him his evil temper still slept like a wicked giant, waiting only to be aroused.

Then one day Mother was getting school clothes ready for Mike and Jackie, his younger sister. Nancy, the baby, toddled everywhere, laughing and gurgling. Mike's dump truck sat on the upstairs porch.

Suddenly everybody heard the breaking of glass out on the porch. Baby Nancy had been there. Mother rushed up to see whether she was hurt. Mike thought of his truck and ran to the porch too. What he saw when he got there was little Nancy sitting on the floor with a piece of wood in her hand and hitting the new truck with all her baby strength, laughing all the time.

The windshield was battered down flat against the hood, and the glass lay scattered all around on the floor. One of the headlights was broken.

Mike let out a howl of anger, dashed to the baby, pushed her aside, and grabbed the truck.

"Mike!" Mother cried. "Mike!"

Mike's black brows were drawn down, and it seemed as if forked lightning flashed from his eyes. He ran to the edge of the upstairs porch, raised his arms, and with all his strength, hurled his truck to the sidewalk far below. Mother and Jackie ran to the edge and looked down, while the baby sobbed piteously, "Mikie hu't Nancee."

The truck was smashed beyond repair.

Mike burst into a torrent of tears and ran to his room. Mother followed him. "Do you know, Mike, your truck could have been repaired? The company that made it sells spare parts. Your father bought the catalog. And poor baby! She meant no harm. She is so little."

Mike felt weak after his temper fit, and he worried what Father would say if he came home and saw what he had done. So he got a cardboard box and picked up the broken truck. He carried it to the basement and hid it behind the furnace.

He decided then and there to fight his enemy and conquer it. Every time he felt a spell of fury coming on, he would think of the furnace and the truck in the box behind it.

Three months went by with no violent outbursts. One day Mike and Father were cleaning the basement.

"What's this?" Father asked, pulling the box out, now covered with dust and ashes. He opened it and saw the ruined truck.

"I guess my temper's in there," Mike said, tears in his eyes. "My mean temper. It's in that box. I don't want to see it again."

Father understood. He had forgotten about the truck and had not missed it; but he had noticed his son's efforts to be good.

Mike's shoulders shook with sobs. The beautiful truck had meant so much to him, and he himself had destroyed it. He could blame no one but himself. "I guess," he said, his voice trembling a little, "I guess I've got something now better than a dump truck."

"You have, son," Father said proudly. "You certainly have. You have a truckload of victory."

11
Rashid's Broken Vow
by Goldie Down

Rashid stood in front of the small piece of cracked mirror propped against the bathroom wall and straightened his tie. He stooped so he could see to check his hair. Every black, shiny wave was in place. He looked down. Suit pressed? Shoes cleaned? Yes. He was ready to begin the day.

Rashid was a student colporteur in India. The colporteur leader had stressed again and again to the students that their clean, neat appearance was "half the battle" when they knocked on doors trying to sell their books. Rashid had a wide smile that revealed gleaming white teeth, and that added another 25 percent to his chances of taking orders.

For nearly two weeks Rashid had been working on his own in the great city of Agra. He had had some successes and many failures, but all in all he was doing quite well, and he certainly had hopes of earning that scholarship he needed.

Before leaving the room, Rashid patted his chest to reassure himself that the cloth pouches were in place. Slung over his shoulders under his coat, these pouches held books and tracts. Prospectus, pencil, and order pad were all hidden from the sight of the prospective customer, according to the custom of Seventh-day Adventist colporteurs in 1946.

"Where will I go this morning?" Rashid asked himself as he mounted his bicycle. Besides other smaller books, he was selling sets of *Uncle Arthur's Bedtime Stories* imported from America, so it was no use going to poor people who would not know how to read English. He had to concentrate on fine, big homes, in which he knew well-educated people would live.

He rode aimlessly down the road for about a mile until he saw a notice: "Cantonment Area." Rashid's eyes brightened. There would be many well-educated Indians and even some Europeans in the military area. No use going to the troops' quarters, of course; he would go to the bungalows where the officers lived.

Humming a little tune, he turned his bicycle in at the first gateway. A sentry stood there, but people were always going in and out through the gate, and he took no special notice of Rashid. The colporteur sped down the smooth, black roadway between avenues of gorgeous shade trees. He saw big notices here and there: "A. Coy. Mess" or "A. Coy. S.P." Rashid didn't know what they meant, and after a while he didn't even bother to read them anymore.

Now, where would the officers' quarters be? He had no idea, but there was a fine-looking building up ahead, and he could ask directions there.

With his eyes fixed on the building Rashid almost fell off his bicycle with fright when a military police officer (MP) dashed out onto the road and stopped him.

"Where d'you think you're going, boy?" he demanded sternly.

"I don't know. I mean, where do the officers live around here?" Rashid stammered.

Given time to think, he could speak quite acceptable English, but now he was so shocked that he stuttered and stammered as he tried to explain that he had come to sell religious books to the army officers.

The MP eyed him even more sternly. "You'd better tell that yarn to the lieutenant colonel," he said. Taking hold of Rashid's bicycle with his big left hand, he led the way toward the fine building. His right hand hovered suggestively near his belt, from which hung holsters that Rashid figured must contain some fearsome weapon. There was no way of escape. There was nothing he could do but march along in front of the officer.

As they drew nearer to the fine building, Rashid could see that it was an office of some kind. Uniformed messengers darted here and there; the shimmer of glass and polished wood desks with piles of papers was visible through the half-open windows.

His companion halted at the foot of the steps and saluted smartly. "Caught this young fellow trespassing, sir," he said to an officer seated at a desk just outside the door.

"Oh?" the officer stopped his writing. "What are you doing in here?" he said to Rashid. "Don't you know this is a prohibited area? Can't you read the signboards?"

"No, sir. Yes, sir." Rashid gulped nervously. "I came in to sell books, sir." He went to put his hand under his coat to draw out his prospectus as proof that he was telling the truth, but the officer roared at him, and at the same instant the MP grabbed his arm. Apparently they thought he had a weapon hidden under his coat.

"Take him in to the lieutenant colonel," the officer said. "Let him tell his story there."

Rashid was marched into the lieutenant colonel's office and stood silently by the officer's desk as the MP explained what had happened.

The lieutenant colonel was a very busy man, and this interruption in his already tight schedule made him annoyed. "What's your excuse?" he demanded. "There are plenty of notices around. Why did you come into this prohibited area?"

The more Rashid tried to tell his reason and explain why he had not seen the notices and that he had come only to sell books, the more angry the officer became.

"Sell books!" he roared. "Religious books, children's books . . . to us! Tell the truth, boy!"

When Rashid protested that he *was* telling the truth, the officer became furious. "Search him," he directed, "and have him put in the lockup until he decides to tell the truth."

An armed guard appeared and led Rashid to a small room with a tiny barred window. Expertly he ran his hands over Rashid's clothing. "Hey, what's this?" he demanded when he felt the bulging pouch of books under Rashid's coat. "Take your coat off, young'un, and let's see what you've got there."

"It's only my books," Rashid explained. "I told you I am a book seller."

"Then why have you got them hidden under your coat?" The guard eyed the boy suspiciously. "If they're good books, as you say, why are you hiding them?"

"I'm not hiding them," Rashid protested. "It's not hiding; it's a-a-a sales technique. So as not to frighten the customer when he sees so many books all at once. I show them one at a time."

"H'mmm." The guard was still suspicious. "*Toward a Better Day,*" he read aloud. "That sounds mighty like something a political party would print." He glowered at Rashid.

"No, it's religious. It's about the Bible."

The guard went through the books one by one, opening them carefully and leafing through each one in search of a hidden weapon or secret information. Clearly he was very disappointed when he found nothing that he could use to prove Rashid was a spy. He shook out the empty pouch. "Here," he called to a messenger, "carry all these books outside and pile them up somewhere. The lieutenant colonel will have to see them later when he has time."

He glared at Rashid. "All right, boy, you can sit down." The guard went out, slamming the door behind him and locking it with a great jangle of keys.

Rashid sat down on a small stool, the only furniture in the room. His legs felt weak and shaky. Now what sort of mess was he in? What could he do to convince these army officers that he was telling the truth? If only Pastor A. E. Nelson were here, perhaps he could help to convince them. Rashid brightened a little. If he could get word to Pastor Nelson, he felt sure everything would be all right. Pastor Nelson was an American missionary, but he had spent 30 years in India and could speak the language and knew the customs. Yes, everything would be all right if only Pastor Nelson could come.

Rashid felt in his pocket for the stub of pencil he always carried in case he lost his order pencil. Now, if only he had a scrap of paper. The guard had taken his hidden bags of books from him and made him empty his pockets of anything suspicious before he had thrust him into the room. But there was an old envelope in his inside pocket. He had overlooked that pocket when the guard was demanding his possessions.

Resting the paper on the smooth concrete floor, he scribbled a little note. "Dear Pastor Nelson, I've been arrested by mistake. I'm in the cantonment prison. Can you come and help me?" Then he carefully signed his name, "Rashid Morris Massey."

Folding the envelope, Rashid stepped to the door and looked through the small barred opening. The guard was standing a few paces away. Rashid beckoned him over.

"Could you please send this note to my employer?" he asked. "He lives only—" Before he could finish his sentence the guard tore the note from his hand and snapped, "No, can't be done. You're held as a spy suspect."

Rashid went slowly back to his stool and sat down heavily. "A spy suspect." So they thought he was a spy. That explained why the lieutenant colonel had acted so furious.

Lieutenant Colonel Barkly was a Muslim. Rashid had seen that at a glance; and he, Rashid, looked like a Hindu. There was a great deal of unrest simmering between Muslims and Hindus in those days. A year after this story happened, the Muslims and Hindus were to settle the problem by dividing the land of India into two separate countries: Pakistan for the Muslims, and India for the Hindus. But Rashid did not know that then. All he knew was that it was a serious offense to be even suspected of spying for either side.

What could he do? What if the lieutenant colonel never believed his story? What would happen to him? A spy. Spies were taken out and shot at dawn, weren't they? Rashid shuddered. How had he gotten into this mess?

"Lord, please get me out of it," he prayed. He had been silently lifting his heart to God for help ever since the MP had stopped him. Now his muddled thoughts took on definite shape. "Get me out of it, Lord. Please make them believe me; and just get me out of this mess, Lord, and I'll never go canvassing again. Please help me, Lord."

Poor Rashid. He was so worried and frightened. Every minute seemed an hour, and every hour an eternity as he sat there in the little guardroom wondering what was going to happen to him next.

Boom, boom, boo-oom. The sentry was banging out the hour on his brass gong. Mechanically Rashid counted the strokes. "Ten, eleven, twelve." Noon! No wonder he felt weak. He was hungry now, as well as frightened. By this time of day he should have taken one or two orders and been home again for food and rest, getting ready to start in again about 4:00, when everyone had recuperated from the fierce midafternoon heat.

"Here, boy!" The guard called in through the little window as his key grated in the lock. Again Rashid was led before the lieutenant colonel. The passage of hours had not improved the man's temper. Perhaps he too was feeling hungry.

"Speak up, boy," he ordered Rashid. "What were you doing in here? Who sent you? Why were you looking for the officers' houses?"

Again Rashid tried to explain, only to be interrupted by the lieutenant colonel's roar. "Tell the truth! Selling books, bah! You'll be punished all the worse for telling such lies." An angry wave of his hand signified that Rashid was to be taken back to the lockup while the officer went home to lunch.

When he reached his home the lieutenant colonel was still fuming about the boy who was trying to tell him such an outrageous story. "Such impudence," he said to his wife as he told her about it.

"What is he like?" his wife asked as she poured iced water into a glass and handed it to him. "Tell me all about it while the servant brings the meal in. Do you really think he's a Hindu spy?"

Between long gulps of iced water the lieutenant colonel told his wife all about the boy who had come so boldly cycling into a forbidden area of the cantonment and then had given him such an unlikely story as the reason for his being there.

"Did you see his books?" questioned his wife.

"I don't think he had any," declared her husband. "I asked the MP whether he had an attaché case or a bag of any kind with him. He said he hadn't seen any."

"Did the boy say what sort of books he was selling?"

"Yes, he kept saying they were religious books of some sort—or children's books. I didn't take much notice of that part of his story."

"Oh, dear." His wife was struck by a sudden memory. "I think you've made a big mistake. He's a good boy."

Her husband stared at her.

"Yes," she continued. "About a week ago a very smart, clean-looking boy came here selling books. They were imported books for children and very expensive; but they had lovely pictures and stories in them. I bought the whole set of 20 from him for our children. It sounds to me as if it is the same boy that you've caught."

"Could be," her husband admitted a bit sheepishly. "Come to think of it, he didn't really look wicked, only terribly frightened."

"He'd have cause to be frightened if you shouted at him, dear." His wife smiled fondly at him.

"Would you know him again—the boy who sold you the books?"

"Yes, I'm sure I would. I think I even have his name here somewhere. He signed the receipt when I gave him the money for the books."

The lieutenant colonel went to the front door and barked an order to his driver. The man saluted and immediately swung the huge station wagon around and started back to the office.

"Lieutenant colonel wants you." The guard opened the door of the little room and accompanied Rashid out to the station wagon. "Get in," he ordered as Rashid hesitated.

Rashid climbed into the back seat of the car. His legs felt like jelly. *Now where are they taking me?* he wondered desperately. He felt even more frightened now than he had all morning, if that was possible.

Presently the car turned into a long driveway. *Those red-blossomed trees!* Rashid's heart leaped. *That beautiful bungalow! I've been here before.* Frantically he searched his memory. Had he received an order at this house or not?

The car drew up, and the driver nodded to him to get out. A uniformed servant led him into the sitting room, and Rashid felt a surge of relief mingle with his fear. Yes, he had sold books here. He remembered that the woman had smiled and welcomed him graciously. At first he had mistaken her for a European because she was so fair and spoke such beautiful English. They had talked for a long time, and she had liked his books and bought them.

Now Rashid turned on his brightest smile and spoke very politely as the woman entered the room. He didn't know what it was all about, but he had a feeling that all would turn out well.

"You must be hungry," the gracious woman said to Rashid. "I'll tell the servant to prepare some food for you."

As her husband came into the room, she said, "It is the same boy."

Rashid froze when he saw the lieutenant colonel, but that gentleman smiled at him. "My wife is vouching for you, young man. She says she bought some books from you. I'm sorry I mistook your identity this morning."

Almost beside himself with relief, Rashid said that it was quite all right, that it didn't matter now, and with general apologies and explanations all around, friendly relations were assumed.

The colonel and his wife withdrew to eat in the dining room, and a little table was set up in the sitting room for Rashid. Caste and religious differences prevented them from eating together.

After the meal the lieutenant colonel came back into the room. "My wife says I ought to make amends for wasting your whole morning by buying some of your books for the company library. Have you got anything that would be suitable?"

"Yes, sir," Rashid answered quickly.

"All right, then. You may go now. Here's my card. Bring this with you and come to my office this afternoon at 5:00 p.m. and show me your samples."

"Thank you, sir. But what about my bicycle, sir? It's at your office, sir."

"H'mmm, yes, I suppose it is." Turning to his wife, he asked, "Could the mali go and fetch it?"

"Yes, it won't take long. Sit down and wait here. Please excuse us; we have an appointment now."

In a short time the servant appeared riding Rashid's bicycle and handed it over to the boy. Thankfully Rashid took it and rode back to the mission.

But more was still to come.

Another thing their leader had impressed on the student colporteurs was to be punctual. Accordingly Rashid set out in good time, and using the lieutenant colonel's card as his magic wand, he was ushered into the great man's office on the tick of 5:00.

The guard produced the confiscated pouch of books, and with a prayer on his lips Rashid began his canvass.

Perhaps the lieutenant colonel was more eager to make amends than he was interested in the books, but in a short time he had ordered 120 rupees' worth of books for the army library.

Of course, after that experience Rashid didn't give up canvassing, despite his vow. How could he? He went on working and praying until he became a star colporteur and a publishing department secretary. He never tires of telling other canvassers the story of the wonderful way in which God turned evil into good.

12
Josie and the Hand-me-down
by Dorothy Aitken

"I hate it! I hate it! I'll never wear it!" Josie flung the brown dress onto the bed and slouched into a chair. "Why do I always have to wear Ella May's hand-me-downs? Why can't I ever have anything new—something I can pick out myself?" Josie immediately wished she hadn't said all that when she saw the troubled expression on Mother's face.

"Oh, I know," Josie went on. "I suppose it is the best I can do right now, but I am so tired of Ella May's things—Ella May's winter coat, Ella May's ski outfit, Ella May's formal, Ella May's tartan skirt. Of course, they are beautiful and expensive—all of Ella May's things are—and they are hardly worn at all, but . . ." Josie's sigh was something akin to pain. "I'd like to be able to pick out my own things for once, even if they don't come from Sandstrom's."

Mother walked over to the window and looked out. "I wish you could have the things you want, Josie," she began softly, "but you know how things are right now. Ever since Daddy quit working on the Sabbath, he has had a hard time. He also feels bad that you can't have all the nice things you want, particularly since you are going away to school. But this can't last forever. He'll find work soon, I'm sure."

Josie bit her lip. She knew her outburst was out of place, particularly at a time when the family was having to pull together.

"You know," Mother went on, "you are mighty lucky to have Ella May for a cousin. I don't know what you would take to school with you if she hadn't given you these lovely things."

"That's another thing, Mother." Josie got up and joined her mother at the window. "Ella May feels so . . . so . . . well, so uppity about it all. I heard Aunt Betty tell you the other day that if Daddy and you hadn't joined that crazy religion, they wouldn't have to be helping us."

"I hoped you wouldn't let that bother you." Mother sighed. "We are certain we are doing what is right, and what others say should not concern us or make us unhappy. You know," she added after a pause, "that brown dress is actually an answer to prayer."

"An answer to prayer! That?" Josie picked up the brown dress and looked at it appraisingly. "Mother, that's not an answer to prayer. I hate brown."

Mother took the dress and held it against the girl. "Look in the mirror, dear. Brown is a very good color for you. With your brown eyes and brown hair, a brown dress goes very nicely. And this bright, hand-stitched embroidery, if you will notice, sets it off beautifully."

"It's a fine dress and all that," Josie conceded, "but it still is a hand-me-down. I'll never be able to forget that. And just why you would call it an answer to prayer, I'll never figure out."

"You have no idea, Josie, how many nights lately I have lain awake wondering what we would be able to get you for a Sabbath dress to take to school. With things like they are right now, there just isn't money for a Sabbath dress. But, you know, one night last week I got to thinking about Ella May and all her clothes, some of which she almost never wears, and I prayed that God would impress Ella May to give you something suitable for a Sabbath dress. And this is it," she ended, putting the dress back on the hanger and straightening the collar.

Josie was silent as she took the dress and hung it in the closet. "I'm sorry, Mother," she said. "You know I'll wear it and try to be happy, even though I don't like it. But no boy will ever look at me twice in that thing. Now, now," she held up a restraining hand, "you don't have to say it. 'Be sweet and friendly and share, and you will have friends whatever you wear.' " She laughed. "I've heard that so many times—I hardly think I can forget it."

So Josie went away to school with her hand-me-down wardrobe, as she called it. Several weeks passed, and she was surprised at the compliments she got whenever she wore the brown dress. "It's just an old, brown hand-me-down," she would say to herself as she stood in front of the mirror, "and I'll always hate it."

One Saturday night Josie and her roommate, Marge, were sitting in the academy gym watching the others march. Both girls had done several marches with various boys and had decided to sit this one out. Suddenly Josie grabbed Marge by the arm. "See that tall boy marching with Angie over on the other side of the gym? Look. He's scratching his nose right now. See him?"

"Sure, I see him. That's Bernie, and he's a senior, a junior elder in the church, on the honor roll every term, and in everything. What about him?"

"He's going to ask me to march with him tonight."

Marge's eyes got big. "Whatever gave you that idea?"

"Why, he said 'Good morning' to me in the hall last night."

"And you think he likes you just because he said 'Good morning' to you? How crazy can you get?"

"Listen, stupid, he said 'Good morning' to me last night. Don't you get it?"

"You mean you had him so shook that he said 'Good morning' when it was night? Well, you might have something there."

"Of course I do. Wait till the music stops. He's been trying all evening to get up the nerve to ask me."

"How do you know?" Marge asked.

"Oh, I just know." Josie shrugged.

So when Josie saw Bernie start across the gym in her direction, her heart gave a couple of flip-flops, and she automatically smoothed her hair with one hand.

"Care to march?" Bernie's voice sounded deeper than she thought it was, and she noticed before she looked up at him that the toes of his shoes had a spit-and-rub polish, even though they were obviously worn.

Around and around the gym they marched. Then, just before they sat down, Bernie said with an appraising look, "Did anyone ever tell you how stunning you look in that brown dress?"

Josie caught her breath and looked down at the embroidery on the cuffs. "Oh, it's the same old thing I wear every week. I'm sure people are getting tired of seeing me in it."

"Well, I'm not. Ever since the first time I noticed you in that dress, I haven't been able to take my eyes off you. It's stunning on you. Suits your coloring exactly."

Josie blushed a bit.

All too soon the evening was over and Josie wondered if Bernie would ever see her again, or was he just flattering her? But at the door of the girls' dorm she heard him say, "How about going with me to the film next Saturday night—in the brown dress, of course?"

Years later on the day of their wedding Josie heard Bernie say, "Darling, you're beautiful, but no more so than you were in that gorgeous brown dress back in the academy."

13
When No One Pursues Them
by Penny Estes Wheeler

For several minutes Winnie stood in front of her dormitory room mirror, watching the serious face reflected there. At last she gave her short, dark hair a final swipe with the hairbrush and turned to face her sister. "I guess I look OK," she said, frowning.

"Silly! You look fine," her sister Hildy replied. "I don't know why you're making such a big deal of this."

Winnie bent down to straighten her nylons. "Big deal," she said. "I get a call from the assistant principal to come to his office, and you think it's not a big deal."

"Mr. Roberts is a nice man. I can't recall his ever biting any student," Hildy laughed.

"Yes, but he's campus-bound them or something. Trouble is, I can't imagine what he wants with me. My grades are all right, and I don't date often enough to have a problem about a boy, and I'm just a junior, so it couldn't be about graduation, and—"

"Why don't you just trot right out the door and across the campus and find out what he wants?" Hildy interrupted.

"Oh," Winnie squealed. "It's 10:00, and I'm supposed to be there right now. Meet me at lunch." Grabbing her notebook, she flew from the room.

Slowing down as she approached the ad building, Winnie made her shaking legs carry her down the hall to the registrar's office. "I have an appointment with Mr. Roberts," she told Sue, the student receptionist.

Sue glanced down at the phone on the desk. With a motion toward the lighted button on the phone, she said, "He's busy right now. I'll let you know when you can see him."

Winnie stood at the counter trying not to stare at Sue or Mrs. Iwanski, the registrar, seated at a desk on the other side of the room. Sue stacked a sheet of typing paper, a carbon sheet, and a yellow sheet together and placed them in the typewriter, adjusting the margins. She turned and

50

caught Winnie's eyes. "You may sit down on the bench by the wall if you like. I'll call you."

Winnie sat. She studied her fingernails; one needed a file badly. She opened her notebook and tried to review her biology notes. *The grasshopper's body is divided into three parts: head, thorax, and abdomen . . . So what?* she thought.

A middle-aged man walked past, nodding to her. The industrial ed teacher . . . She couldn't remember his name.

"Mr. Roberts will see you now."

Startled, Winnie jumped. She closed her notebook and slowly walked the few yards to the assistant principal's office. Her knock sounded feeble at his open door.

Mr. Roberts stood up, all six-foot-three of him. "Come in, come in," he said, his voice filling the office and rumbling down the hall. He put out his hand. "How are you, Winnie?"

"Fine. Thank you."

"Well, have a seat. Right there. That's fine. Beautiful weather, isn't it? There's nothing like a day in May."

Winnie nodded. "You asked to see me?"

"Ah, yes." Mr. Roberts picked up a folder on his desk. The words "Neff, Winnie" stared at the girl from its corner.

"Fact is," Mr. Roberts began, "we need another girl for our registrar's office. You aren't working now." It was a statement more than a question.

"No. I worked in the cafeteria all last semester, but—"

He laughed, waving the folder. "I have it all here. Your grades are good, except you might do a bit better in algebra. You've had typing and got a final grade of A. The dean of women recommends you. Would you like the job?"

"Why, yes. Yes, sir. Oh, I have afternoon classes."

"This would be mornings from 8:00 to 12:00. No Sunday work unless you wanted to help out an afternoon girl."

"I'd love it!" Winnie gasped. "I need to work, and I want to."

"Good." Mr. Roberts leaned back in his chair, idly leafing through her folder. "Tell you the truth, it's a special job—working in the office. We went through the files of all the girls who aren't working and many who are. Your typing ability and your schedule helped us to ask you. But a more important factor is your reputation."

"Oh?"

"Of course. This is an important position. The work must be done with accuracy. Recording grades, for example. A mistake there can lower a student's GPA and perhaps jeopardize their chance of attending college. Just as important is the necessity of keeping everything that goes through this office confidential. We don't release a student's grade to another student, and we don't release the reason a student is campus-bound. In other words, everything in the files for the 300 students we have this year is confidential, and everything in the files of previous students is also. You never give out information without the permission of Mrs. Iwanski or the principal or me."

Winnie nodded. "Yes, sir. I understand. I'm just thrilled you chose me."

Mr. Roberts stood up. "I know we'll be pleased with your work. Now, I'll officially introduce you to Mrs. Iwanski, and she'll show you around."

Winnie's heart sang as the motherly woman showed her the vault, the current student files, the grade files, the class absence files, the corner for duplicating work. So much to remember.

Sue's reception was friendly, if formal, toward her new coworker. Halfway through Winnie's tour of the compact office, a tall, well-tanned girl came bouncing in. "Oh, Mrs. I., I'm sorry I'm so late. That dentist was supposed to take me at 8:00, but he was late, and—oh, we're getting a new girl?"

Winnie smiled as Mrs. Iwanski drew her forward. "Meet Jolinda," she said. "Jolinda Peterson, Winnie Neff. She'll be working mornings with us."

Then to Winnie, "Jolinda is our transcript girl. She spends most of her time in the duplicating nook."

"Welcome aboard," Jolinda said. "Sorry to come bursting in on you. Had to get a tooth filled, and he drilled a half hour, no lie. I'm still dead on one side. Am I talking funny? Can't feel my tongue."

Winnie described her morning to Hildy over lentil loaf and creamed cauliflower. "Mr. Roberts is so loud that he's always scared me silly. But he's friendly, and, well, he said so many nice things to me. I just hope I can do the job."

"Sure you can," Hildy said. "If they have confidence in you, at least have confidence in yourself. What girls will you be working with?"

"Jolinda Peterson—"

"She's a riot," Hildy laughed. "We have gym together."

"That must be an experience," Winnie giggled. "She seems like such a nut. And Sue Somebody-or-other works at the front desk."

"Sue who?"

"I didn't get her last name. She's tall, dresses quite stylishly. Even had on nylons and heels at work. Blond hair, turned in a flip."

"Sue Reynolds, I'll bet." Hildy took a swallow of milk. "Is she kind of stuck-up?"

"We-ll, she's just rather formal and distant and terribly efficient."

"That's Sue! She rode in the taxi with us when we went to town a couple of weeks ago. Had green lines drawn on her eyelids," Hildy added as an afterthought.

Winnie soon gained confidence in her ability as an office worker and thoroughly enjoyed it. Every hour she collected absence slips from each classroom, then recorded each student's absence on their card. At the end of the day she typed a list of all absences for Mrs. Iwanski. In between collecting slips, she filed and did odd bits of typing for the registrar. The stack of items to be filed never ran out, and sometimes it was hard to keep from pausing to read letters in the students' files. The fact that everything was confidential made even the dullest fact seem exciting to the three girls.

Jolinda had the personality of a friendly, good-natured puppy. Nothing bothered her, and she had fun with everything she did. With Sue's aloofness and Winnie's shyness, Jolinda injected life into the otherwise quiet office.

Sue remained an untouchable china doll. Since it was her second year in the office, she knew everything there was to know about office procedure. Oh, she talked to Jolinda and Winnie; she was congenial, but never really friendly. Sue kept everyone at arm's length and surrounded herself with an aura of mystery. She didn't join in the girlish banter of her coworkers. She never giggled, and her smile rarely reached her eyes. She had little to do with Jolinda and Winnie until . . .

Sue stood at the current files, slowly fitting little blue grade slips into each folder. Mrs. Iwanski was in the committee room taking the minutes of a long meeting. Jolinda stood at her machine making copies of transcripts, and Winnie sat at Mrs. I.'s desk typing a test for Mr. Roberts.

It was cold outside, and the artificial heat made the office too warm. A quiet, dull day.

"Hey, you two," Sue called in a loud whisper. "Come here."

"One sec," Jolinda said.

Winnie finished typing a multiple-choice question and then stood, stretching her taut back muscles before going to Sue.

"Whatcha got there?" Jolinda asked.

Sue held up a long, white, sealed envelope. "This bugs me. Really bugs me," she said.

"What?" Winnie asked.

Jolinda took the envelope and read the capital letters typed across its face: "DO NOT OPEN WITHOUT PERMISSION OF R. E. ALLEN, PRINCIPAL."

"That's from Charlie Aptley's file," Winnie said. "I've noticed it before."

"Right," Sue retorted, "and the envelope says not to open without Elder Allen's permission. What I want to know is what's so important that it must be kept sealed unless the academy principal gives his permission?"

"It's really none of our business," Winnie said, turning back toward her typing.

"She's right," Jolinda agreed. "You ought to put it back."

"We're responsible girls, or they wouldn't have hired us for this job," Sue insisted. "If we told everything we know, we wouldn't work here."

"*Responsible!* Exactly why you should put it back," Jolinda told her.

"Look, I've seen this thing a hundred times, and Mrs. I.'s always around," Sue said. "For once the dear woman's not here, and *I'm* going to find out Charlie's secret."

Winnie turned around. "It's not our business. We're trusted not to—"

"We'll never have another chance," Sue insisted, taking the envelope into the duplicating nook. "We can seal it back so no one can tell it's been opened."

Sue carefully laid the envelope on the counter, then slid a letter opener under the flap. She worked slowly. "Almost got it," she breathed, then, "Oh, no . . . I tore it!"

Winnie jumped up to join the two girls. "Oh, Sue. How could you?" she wailed.

"Just what are you going to do now?" Jolinda demanded.

"I'll think of something." She removed the letter and scanned it.

"Hey, listen. Charlie was picked up with a lot of other kids who had marijuana on them. Doesn't say if he was smoking it. Well, that doesn't surprise me a bit. Look at the way he dresses." Suddenly she clapped her hand over her mouth. "You'd better not tell a soul."

"As if we were the ones who opened the envelope in Charlie's file." Winnie stormed to Hildy that night. "I tell you, Sue talked more today than she has all year, and I much prefer her quiet."

"So what did you do about the torn envelope?"

"Put the whole thing in the back of her bottom drawer. Now she'll have to get into the principal's secretary's office somehow and get an envelope and use their typewriter."

"Even use their typewriter?"

"Yes," Winnie moaned. "It's an electric and types differently from ours."

Winnie flopped onto her bed and hugged her stuffed rabbit. "Tell you the truth, the whole thing has made me a little sick."

"*You* didn't open the envelope," Hildy protested. "You didn't even read it."

"I might as well have. If Elder Allen or even Mrs. Iwanski discovers it gone, it won't matter that I was only a listener." She sighed. "If only Mr. Roberts hadn't made such a big thing about trusting me."

Hildy lowered her voice to a stage whisper. "So what did the letter say?" she giggled.

Winnie didn't appreciate the joke. "Don't start that," she retorted. "I don't even want to think about what it said, much less tell you."

With considerable fear Winnie went to work the next morning. But to her relief, Mrs. Iwanski didn't seem suspicious and Mr. Roberts didn't seem any different. She had a scare when Elder Allen came down and asked for some information, but he left without going near the files. Somehow Winnie made it through the morning. And the next day. And the next.

"It's terrible," Winnie reported to her sister as the girls got ready for bed. "Elder Allen stopped by again today, and I froze. Jolinda acted more flighty than usual, and even Sue had trouble being her old smooth self."

"You shouldn't act so guilty," Hildy said, her words obstructed by hairpins. "Act guilty, and they'll wonder why."

"How can I help it? I feel guilty because I *am* guilty. Elder Allen's so friendly. He comes in with something to show us, and we act like he's a cop ready for the capture. I tell you, it's surprising what guilt feelings make you do."

"How about going and telling him about it? Or Mrs. Iwanski?"

"Never. I mean, Sue and Jolinda wouldn't do it, and actually, what good would it do? Then they wouldn't trust us, and to tell the truth, these past few days have made Jolinda and me a lot more honest than we were."

"And Sue?"

"She doesn't say much, but she's worried. Mrs. Iwanski was checking senior GPAs this morning. Charlie's too, of course."

Hildy shook her head. "I'm still curious about what was in that envelope. You've just got to get it back into his folder in some way."

"Don't I know it," Winnie sighed.

Winnie and Hildy hurried into the worship room the next evening to see Elder Allen sitting on the platform—the speaker for the night. Hildy gave Winnie a questioning nudge, and her sister shook her head. "No, not yet," she whispered.

The girls sat down, and Winnie caught Sue's eye across the room. Sue slid her finger across her throat in a cutting motion. Winnie heard nothing that the principal said.

Sleep came slowly that night. Winnie pounded her pillow and finally threw it on the floor.

"Aren't you asleep yet?" Hildy asked, half cross with sleepiness.

"Not yet." Winnie sat up and pulled the blankets under her chin. "Know what, Hildy?"

"What?"

"Mr. Jenkins quoted Proverbs 28:1 in class today."

Hildly yawned. "He did?"

"It was something like the wicked flee when no man pursues them."

"And?"

"Don't you get it? That's all I keep thinking about. When you're guilty of something, you think everyone's after you. Every time Mrs. I. goes near the files, we practically turn to stone. Elder Allen's been coming in our office every day, and we like him. He kids around with us, you know; he's a lot of fun. But now we can't even look at him—not even Sue. We're so scared that he's found out."

Hildy rose to her knees to pull up her bedspread. "I'll wager it's a hot day in the tundra before you girls pull such a fool stunt again."

"You'd better believe it. I'll throw myself across the envelope if Sue even tries such a thing."

Hildy laughed. "If that's the case, Winnie the Pooh, you'd better get some sleep to build up your strength."

Eight o'clock the next morning found the three girls outside the office door waiting for the business manager to unlock it. "Listen, you two," Winnie whispered, "we've got to get that letter back in the file today."

"We've tried all week," Sue snapped. "Elder Allen's secretary never leaves her desk."

"Well, I had a terrifying dream last night," Winnie said. "Elder Allen found out and had us at the long table where they have citizenship committee."

"I dreamed about it too," Jolinda admitted. "Actually, I just thought about it all night." She stopped talking as the business manager came with the key.

"I can't imagine how we let you do such a dumb thing," she continued to Sue as they got inside. "I've always been proud that they trusted me." She took off her coat to hang it up. "I've never been so miserable as I've been these past few days. So help me, I doubt if I even ever read someone else's absence slip again."

Sue smoothed her eyebrow with a carefully manicured fingernail. "Actually, I had a brainstorm about 5:00 this morning."

"What?"

"It better be better than your last one."

"Well, as we know, Mrs. I. doesn't come in till around 10:00 on Friday because she has her hair done, and I'm about positive that Miss Fields goes to the beauty shop too this morning."

Jolinda nodded. "Yes, she does. Once, I needed to ask her something, and she didn't come in till 9:30 or so."

"The problem is that Elder Allen might be in," Winnie said. "Won't he think it strange that we're using his secretary's typewriter?"

"We'll just have to hope he leaves for a few minutes or closes his office door or something," Sue said. "We can't wait another week to get this typed."

"So Elder Allen finally left his office," Winnie whispered to Hildy as they ate lunch. "It was 9:00, and time was running out fast, and I happened to look out the window and saw him going into the library. Sue raced down the hall and had that envelope typed in less than a minute."

"Now you can breathe easy, sleep soundly, and look Elder Allen in the eye," Hildy laughed.

Winnie didn't return her laughter. "I felt so ashamed that I'd have been glad if they'd found out, except that, well, I'm so ashamed that we fell short of the trust they had in us."

"What about Jolinda and Sue?"

"Jolinda feels just as I do." Winnie smiled. "I told her about the wicked running when no one chases them, and she said it described her exactly."

"And Sue?"

"I don't know. You can never tell about her." Winnie shook her head. "We probably could have stopped her if we'd really tried. And I think she feels bad enough that she'd never—"

Just then Sue and Jolinda walked into the cafeteria and straight to Winnie. "I'm going to have a little talk with Elder Allen," Sue said in a tearful voice. "Want to come along?"

Winnie pulled her chair from the table and wordlessly followed the other two girls, a sweet feeling of peace coming into her heart.

The Beginning . . .

1953

The first issue of *Junior Guide* was published in October of 1953.

1964

The word "Junior" was dropped in 1964, when earliteens joined the magazine's reading ranks.

Covers through the decades

1953

1962

1979

1988

1995

2012

Columns and features over the years

On the Trail
Oct. 7, 1953, p. 5

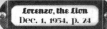
Lorenzo, the Lion
Dec. 1, 1954, p. 24

Andy's Gadget Magic
Aug. 25, 1954, p. 8

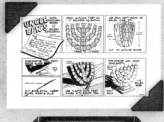

Uncle Ben's Workshop
Oct. 2, 1957, p. 9

Just a Minute with Your Bible
Mar. 18, 1964, p. 22

Morning Watch
April 1, 1964, p. 23

It Happened This Month
Mar. 1, 1972, p. 21

Kitchen Korner
April 13, 1983

Guidelines
Feb. 22, 1986, p. 20

Poetry and stories came from young and old alike.

The back-page facts have been a perennial favorite.

Inside the covers of *Guide*

Pathfinder Can Drive
Oct. 26, 1966, p. 32

Pathfinder Can Drive
Oct. 28, 1970, p. 9

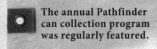

The annual Pathfinder can collection program was regularly featured.

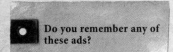

Do you remember any of these ads?

Junior Guide
Oct. 21, 1953, p. 10

Really-Truly Stories
June 5, 1957, p. 23

Choplets
Aug. 24, 1966, p. 31

Games
Aug. 17, 1966, p. 31

Electric Grass Company
Feb. 18, 1976, p. 31

Sabbath School lessons have played an important role in *Junior Guide* and *Guide*.

Sabbath School Lesson
Sept. 12, 1956, p. 22

Sabbath School Lesson
Aug. 12, 1970, p. 25

A letter of congratulations from President Reagan on *Guide's* thirtieth anniversary.

THE WHITE HOUSE
WASHINGTON

October 15, 1982

I appreciate the opportunity to extend my congratulations to the staff and readers of Guide as you celebrate your Thirtieth Anniversary.

As a publication which emphasizes the high ideals of responsibility, obedience, kindness, and good citizenship, Guide has the opportunity to influence people for the good. In stressing the wholesomeness of nature and outdoor activities, Guide reminds its readers of some of life's most important and restorative dimensions.

You have my best wishes on this special year. May you enjoy continued success.

Ronald Reagan

One Really Cool Letter
Jan. 5, 1983, p. 32

Pen Pals
Sept. 10, 1975, p. 21

Pen Pals
Sept. 16, 1981, p. 30

Some readers eventually became husband and wife after first becoming pen pals!

Friends Unlimited
May 18, 1991, p. 7

The Editors

Lawrence Maxwell
1953–1970

Lowell Litten
1971–1983

Penny E. Wheeler
1983–1986

Jeannette Johnson
1986–1994

Carolyn Sutton
1995–1998

Tim Lale
1998–1999

Randy Fishell
2000–

Other ministries

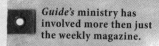

Guide's ministry has involved more then just the weekly magazine.

More Fun
September 1958

Voyager

The Best of Guide

Just Plane Crazy

Guide's Greatest Stories Audio

Guide Web site

Real

Guide's Greatest Stories

14

A Safe Play

by Peggy Hodges

The courthouse was quiet—so quiet that Laurie could hear the occasional buzzing of the electric clock. It was dark outside, although it was only 6:30 in the evening, and the wind that never stopped blowing in the little Western town of Merrill rattled the windows.

There's nothing to be afraid of, Laurie reassured herself. *Everything is locked, and the sheriff's office is right in the next building. It's a little spooky to be the only person in this building, though.*

"At least I hope I'm the only person!" she spoke aloud and giggled nervously as she pulled a copy of the treasurer's report toward her.

She had promised Mr. Baker that it would be ready for the next morning's meeting of the board of commissioners. Laurie was proud of her after-school job at the treasurer's office. At first it had been part of her high school vocational training course, but she had done so well that Mr. Baker had kept her on for the rest of the year. Usually she was through at 5:00 like the rest of the employees, but this report was 12 pages long and difficult to type. She wanted it to be perfect, and the long columns of figures were giving her more than a little trouble. She had gone home for a quick sandwich at 5:00 and then returned, determined to keep her promise to Mr. Baker.

She had never been alone in the huge building before and was acutely aware of the big, old-fashioned walk-in safe in the back of the room. She knew there was more money than usual in it, for that day had marked the deadline for property owners to pay their taxes, and the usual stragglers had come in just before 5:00. She estimated there were several thousand dollars in there now.

The big building next door that housed the sheriff's office also held the county jail, and that brought another problem. She thought nervously of the Indians that were in jail and of how foolish she had been to admit to her classmates that she was afraid of Indians.

Laurie was new in Merrill, coming from a big city in the East, and she had never really seen an Indian until this year. She knew they were the same as everyone else, of course, but it was hard to forget the stories in the history books. She had always pictured Indians burning each other at the stake and torturing the settlers.

There was a big Indian reservation nearby, and the Indians came to town often, especially while Merrill was holding its annual summer festival. The Indians had been a colorful part of the parade, their bronzed skin oiled and gleaming, copper bands shining on their arms and legs. They rode well-groomed Indian ponies, and their princess was a lovely sight, her long black hair reaching the waist of her fringed buckskin robe. She rode proudly at the head of the parade, followed by her people in their ceremonial dress.

Unfortunately, some of the Indians had drunk a little too much "firewater," and Sheriff Olson locked them up until they calmed down. This was an annual occurrence, and the celebrating Indians took the locking up as part of the festival. Because Laurie feared them, the other kids teased her and gave loud war whoops behind her just to see her jump.

She especially hated to see the Indians drink. She knew how alcohol changed the personality of the best of people. Yes, she hated alcohol and she said so. And that was one of the reasons her classmates considered her a bit too prim.

In church school Laurie had been popular, and now she felt deeply hurt to think she was not understood or accepted by her classmates. Perhaps that was why she was so thankful for the work at the treasurer's office. At least it gave her something to do after school.

The sound of the typewriter was loud in the empty room, and she resolutely kept her eyes on the copy, trying to shake off the feeling that she was being watched. She looked apprehensively at the door from time to time and now was startled to see a dim shadow through the frosted glass.

Maybe it was the janitor. No, he would have called out to her, and besides, he cleaned the building early each morning. Who else could get in the outer door? The building was locked securely, and only the employees had keys.

She doggedly kept on typing, then noticed that she had made two errors. She jerked the paper out of the machine, knowing that it was impossible to erase on the slick paper used for the special report.

If only the shadow would move! She could almost picture a feathered war bonnet on it, but knew this was ridiculous. The Indians dressed just like everybody else and acted just the same, too.

Well, she would just go over to the phone and call the sheriff. He'd be there in a minute, and, whoever the intruder was, he couldn't get into the office. The door was locked—or was it? She couldn't remember locking it, but she couldn't imagine not locking it either. She wiped her sweaty hands on her skirt and forced herself to start for the phone.

Suddenly the door swung open, and she whirled to look into the face of a short, stocky man. This was no Indian, but she saw at once that he had been a prisoner. His worn Army surplus fatigues told her that—it was the standard garb at the small jail. He advanced silently toward her, and she backed away.

"Open the safe!" he commanded in a low voice.

Laurie thought of telling him that she didn't know the combination but realized it was useless to lie. Everyone knew that all the employees in the treasurer's office could open the safe.

"I don't remember how," her voice quavered as she answered.

"Don't give me that!" the man barked. "If you don't remember, where do you keep the combination? I know you have it."

"It's in my purse," she admitted, instinctively knowing that her best chance was in stalling for time.

"Get it!" he ordered, his big hairy hand doubled into a threatening fist that seemed more frightening than a gun.

The cruel twist of his thin mouth and the heaviness of his dark jowls were vaguely familiar, and Laurie suddenly remembered where she had seen that face before. On the front page of the newspaper! He was Dick Jerrold, wanted for robbery in a neighboring state. Sheriff Olson had picked him up the week before and was holding him until the proper authorities came for him. She knew he was desperate. Frantic plans for escape shot through her mind as she opened the desk drawer and took out her handbag.

Jerrold grabbed it from her and dumped the contents onto the desk. *What a mess,* she thought as she fumbled through the assortment. She opened various scraps of paper looking for the combination. Finally she gave him one marked "Treasurer's Safe," and he growled, "This had better be the right one, girlie!"

He opened the big outer doors of the safe and bent to fumble with the dial. Laurie watched him from the corner where he had told her to stand. She bent her head and prayed. Who could help her now except the Lord? She knew He would show her what to do but wondered if she would recognize His sign.

Sighing, she glanced up at the clock. It was only 7:00 in spite of the fact that it was so dark. And the past several minutes had seemed hours long.

Then she remembered that Dale Alden, the town marshal, made it a point to check each building to see if it was securely locked. He started in the business section at 6:00 every evening and conscientiously tried each door at the front and rear of each building. Few towns did this anymore, but Merrill seldom changed any of the rituals that had been established for years.

It must be about time for Dale to reach the courthouse, which was one of the last places he checked. The treasurer's office was in a new addition to the building, and she could plainly see the broad front door from the window opposite her. And just then, as if in answer to her feverish thoughts, she saw Dale's big figure coming down the walk. Glancing at Jerrold, she saw that he was still trying the combination, cursing as he started over.

"Please, Lord," she begged as she leaped forward and closed the heavy outer doors of the safe, locking Jerrold inside. Ordinarily she had trouble closing one at a time, but tonight she slammed them both shut. Almost at the same time she undid the wide leather belt from around her waist and hurled it toward the window. The buckle made a loud crash but didn't break the heavy plate glass. It didn't have to. Dale looked up and promptly blew his whistle as he started for the courthouse.

Before she knew it, the place was full of officers, and she was the center of attraction—even more than Jerrold, who was handcuffed and hustled back to his cell. Details of his escape were jumbled, but he had evidently slipped out of jail when the sheriff was called to a disturbance at the festival grounds. He had entered the courthouse through a street window carelessly left open.

Dale held out the scrap of paper Jerrold had dropped. "You'd think an expert like him could open the safe immediately with this combination."

"Well," she admitted, "I can never remember the combination, so I had to write it down, but I marked the one for the post office box 'Treasurer's Safe' and the one for the safe 'Post Office Box.' I didn't want to take a chance on someone getting the safe combination if they found my purse."

"Jerrold got the safe combination, all right!" Dale laughed. "What could have been safer?"

People crowded about the door as Laurie walked out of the building with the marshal. She saw David, one of her classmates, staring at her. He broke into a grin as he said, "I bet you were as scared as if it had been an Indian, huh, Laurie?"

"More scared," she said shakily.

David took her arm and several other boys and girls crowded close.

"We'll walk home with you, Laurie," someone said.

"You look pale," David whispered.

"Any girl as brave as you probably doesn't need protection," added one of the girls. "But we'd like to walk with you anyway."

Laurie hesitated. The report still wasn't done, and she had promised Mr. Baker to have it finished that night. And just when the kids were treating her as though she was one of them.

"Go ahead, Laurie," spoke Mr. Baker. He had joined the throng of interested townspeople. "That report can wait. Even the commissioners will understand why it's late!"

Laurie's sparkle came back as she looked first at him and then at her new friends. The Lord had answered all her prayers at once—Jerrold hadn't harmed her, the kids had accepted her, and, best of all, she had no more fear or prejudice toward Indians.

"Let's go!" she cried happily.

15
For His Own Good
by Lois Mae Cuhel

Mark felt himself becoming impatient with the customer. She had delayed the checker twice by making trips back into the aisles for forgotten grocery items. Now, as Mark stood waiting by her loaded cart, she fumbled for her checkbook and pen. She wrote nervously and became confused about the date. Then she made a mistake about the amount of the check and began again.

Mark looked at the number 2 counter, where he was also responsible for bagging the groceries. Debbie, the checker at number 2, glanced up and signaled with a nod. He left number 1 and bagged quickly. He still had 24 boxes of canned goods to mark and shelve. Mr. Hersh had said to have it done by breaktime, if possible. He looked at his watch. It was going to be hard. He looked back at counter 1. The customer was finally ready.

"I'll be back," he told Debbie.

Mark was energetic and moved fast. In six weeks of after-school work he had impressed Mr. Hersh with his speed and efficiency. And right now he felt resentment toward this customer who was keeping him from doing his job.

The woman stood looking absently about as Mark began pushing her groceries toward the door.

"Oh," she said with a start and followed him.

Mark slowed a bit to let people in through the automatic sliding doors. Then his customer noticed the plant and bulb display that had been set up just inside the entrance.

"What healthy plants!" she exclaimed. As if talking to herself, she went on: "Maybe I could get Ben interested in gardening again. He used to enjoy it . . ."

Mark waited for her to show him where her car was parked. Instead, she began browsing among the plants.

"Could you wait a minute?" she asked. "Would you mind if I just pick out a few of these plants?"

"Yes, I would mind!" Mark blurted out. Then, embarrassed, he made it even worse: "I've got other customers who need their groceries carried out." Red and prickly hot, he heard himself say: "You're not the only customer in the store."

The woman's hand shook as she put the small box of plants back in place. She pressed her lips together, and Mark watched in dismay as her face crumpled and she broke into tears. She clutched her purse and hurried through the doors toward her car. As if in a nightmare, Mark heard Mr. Hersh's voice. He was calling the other carryout boy. "Joe, come over here."

In a lower, tight tone he spoke to Mark. "Let Joe take Mrs. Wynn's groceries out. I want to talk to you in my office."

Mark released the cart to Joe and followed Mr. Hersh. *He must have heard everything,* Mark thought.

Mr. Hersh motioned Mark to sit down opposite his desk. He fixed a steady look on the boy. Mark dropped his eyes and studied the gold-tipped legs of the desk.

"You don't know Mrs. Wynn, do you, Mark?" Mr. Hersh asked.

Mark shook his head.

"No, you wouldn't. Let's see, it's more than two months since she's been in. Let me tell you about Mrs. Wynn, Mark."

Mr. Hersh leaned back in his chair. Mark felt himself forced to look up and listen.

"About two and a half months ago the Wynns were in a serious automobile accident. Both Mr. and Mrs. Wynn were nearly killed. Mrs. Wynn has recovered, but her husband, Ben, is in a state of depression. He's at home now, but he's unable to do very much, and he seems to have lost interest in everything."

Mr. Hersh paused a second. He picked up a pencil and turned it in his fingers.

Ben . . . thought Mark, remembering. *She was thinking about her husband when she said that about the plants.* He tightened his hands together. They were clammy.

"I'm sorry, Mr. Hersh," he said. He wanted to say more, but Mr. Hersh didn't give him time.

"Mark," he said in a tone that allowed no interruption, "I'm going to let you go."

Mark felt dazed and shocked. He had expected a stiff scolding, but not this. Slowly he got to his feet.

"I want you to understand this, Mark. I'm firing you for your own good. I'm taking it upon myself to teach you a lesson that some people never learn. You can't always be sure what lies behind people's behavior. There may be something disturbing them so much, as with Mrs. Wynn, that they're not themselves. And we aren't aware of it. So when we say something sharp or rude to such a person, we're hurting them more than we know."

Mark didn't say anything.

Mr. Hersh put down his pencil and stood up. "Come by and see me tomorrow afternoon, and I'll have your check ready for you. And I'll write a reference to help you get another job."

Mr. Hersh extended his hand. "I'm sorry, Mark."

Mark pretended not to see the outstretched hand. He left without a word. He went out and stood by his bike in back of the supermarket. Fired for his own good, Mr. Hersh had said.

What good? he thought bitterly. *Because I wanted to do my job right. I wanted to be efficient and get things done. I'm usually nice to people. I'm friendly when I have time.*

"When I have time," he said aloud. The words echoed in his mind. They bounced up together with Mr. Hersh's words. "Fired for your own good . . . teach you a lesson about hurting people."

I didn't mean to hurt Mrs. Wynn. I was just concerned about the work and not about her as a person, he thought. *I'll have to do something.*

He turned back to the store. Debbie or Joe might be able to help him. He had to find out Mrs. Wynn's address.

The next day after school Mark stopped at the supermarket to pick up his check.

"Hey, you're late," Joe yelled at him. "Where have you been?"

Mr. Hersh didn't tell him he fired me, I guess, Mark thought.

When Mr. Hersh saw Mark coming, he picked up a check and handed it to him. "Mrs. Wynn called last night, Mark," he said. "She told me what you did."

Mark was surprised. He hadn't expected her to do that.

"Come in and tell me how it went," Mr. Hersh said.

Mark stepped into the office and sat in the same chair he had occupied the day before. This time, however, he sat there with less discomfort.

"Well," he said, "I don't know how to tell it, really. I just kept thinking about what you said, and it seemed like I had to do something." He paused.

Mr. Hersh was listening attentively. "So I bought some plants Mrs. Wynn had been looking at, and I went to her house."

Mark took a deep breath, remembering how he had felt standing at the Wynns' door with the tray of plants in his arms.

"At first Mr. Wynn didn't seem to be paying any attention when we showed him the plants. But Mrs. Wynn persuaded him to come out into the yard with us. She started fixing a place to put them in one of the flower beds. I tried to help, but I didn't know much about planting. After a while I didn't have to help. Mr. Wynn showed me how to tap the plants out of the pots, and a little later on he got down and did some of the planting. I went home after that. Mrs. Wynn wants me to come by on Thursday and help trim some shrubs."

Mark finished the story and stood up. "And that was all there was to it."

Mr. Hersh put his hand on Mark's shoulder. "Well, not quite. Yesterday I told you I had to fire you for your own good. I wanted to teach you a lesson. Today I'd like to hire you for my own good. You've proved to me that you're willing to learn."

Mark was still holding his check in his hand. Mr. Hersh took it from him. "And if you don't mind, I'll keep this until our regular payroll comes around!"

Mr. Hersh laughed, and Mark felt a grin spreading across his own face. "Go take that 'Help Wanted' sign out of the window, and then give Joe a hand. We're getting a little behind around here today."

"Yes, sir!" Mark exclaimed as he hurried toward the sign.

16
Spring Training
by Clare Miseles

"I don't want any pie, Mother," Jennifer said, pushing the plate away. "I'm in training!"

"Training?" Her mother's hands flew up in the air. "You're not really going to join the boys' baseball team, are you?"

"She won't, Mom," Jordy cut in, "because she won't get in!"

"Oh, no?" Jennifer glared at her brother.

"No!"

"Why not? Because I'm a girl?"

"No, because you're not good enough," he told her truthfully.

"But she's a good cook," her dad said, smiling.

"Daddy!" Jennifer cried unhappily.

"But you are!" he said. "God gave you a very good gift."

"Daddy," she sputtered, "g-girls don't just stay home and cook anymore!"

"That's why men are the best cooks in the world," Jordy snickered.

"Then be a cook!" Jennifer snickered back.

"Not my thing," he replied.

"And not my thing, either!" she cried, her brown eyes blazing. "You'll see!" She turned to her parents and waited for them to say something in her favor.

But they didn't say a word. And she so much wanted them to say that the same God who made boys made girls, that He gave them the same gifts, that they were able to do things just as well as boys. Hurt and disappointment clouded Jennifer's round face. The more she thought about it the angrier she became.

That anger didn't leave her, especially when she practiced. She really practiced a lot, too—and hard. After school she hurried home, put on her jeans and sweatshirt and sneakers, piled her long brown hair under an orange baseball cap, and rushed out to meet Kim, her best friend. Kim pitched to her for batting practice, and most of the time Kim's pitching was bad. Sometimes Jennifer would shout, "Who taught you how to pitch?"

Then Kim would get peeved and shout back, "And who taught you how to hit?"

Strangers gathered about to watch, and that made her awfully nervous. One man even cried out, "Your swing is all wrong!"

Mrs. Woolman, a neighbor, didn't help when she thought Jennifer was Jordy. "I should have known it was you by the way you missed the ball," she said, and Jennifer steamed.

But the worst was her brother coming by and standing against the cement wall and watching her. He never said a word, just kept his eyes on her and sometimes shook his head in a kind of sad way. Then did she ever get nervous! Her hands began to sweat, and her swing was way off. The harder she tried, the worse she got. Tears rushed to her eyes, drowning the anger she felt, which wasn't really for anyone but herself. No one had to tell her she wasn't good enough—not Jordy, or anyone. "I'm going to throw in the sponge," she said wearily.

"A sponge is what we'll need." Kim held up her hand. "It's starting to rain."

"Rain?" Jennifer grumbled.

"It's spring," Kim said, walking over to her friend, her eyes full of questions. "Jen, you don't really want to be on the team because you want to play, do you?"

Jennifer sighed and began to walk. Kim followed, shaking the raindrops from her hair. Neither said a word. But a block later Jennifer cleared her throat and squirmed a little. "You're right, Kim," she said. "I don't really want to play. I-I just wanted to show those boys that I have as much right to be on the team as they have. Now I know it isn't just rights—it's what you can do and how well you do it." She sighed deeply, then suddenly brightened. "How about some brownies for your lunch tomorrow?"

Kim smacked her lips. "I love your mom's brownies!"

"My brownies!" Jennifer said. "I'm going to bake some tonight."

"You are?" Kim said slowly. "Is that your thing?"

"Yes," Jennifer smiled, thankful to God for His gifts and happy for the first time in days. "It's just one of my things."

17
Sunshine Inside
by Trudy J. Morgan

Sunshine bands!" I muttered in disgust. I scuffled as quickly as I could from the car to the doors of the nursing home, carrying two stacks of songbooks and bending my head to avoid as much of the rain as I could. I hated Sunshine Bands, but I couldn't tell anyone that. I had organized them.

Yes, it was my fault that all these people were out here today in the rain. Organizing Sunshine Bands was part of my job as youth leader, but it was a part I always wished I could leave to someone else. It always rained this time of year—especially, it seemed to me, on Sabbath afternoons. There didn't seem to be any sunshine to bring to anyone.

Last year our Sunshine Band leader had always gotten up at the beginning of the program and said brightly, "Well, we've come to share some sunshine with you, and since there isn't any outside, we'll make our own sunshine right here inside!" I'd carried on the tradition, but my little speech never convinced me.

The main problem was that just being inside one of these places made me feel gloomy and gray. The feeling stole over me again as I took off my dripping raincoat and looked around the lobby. The furniture was worn and the pictures were, I thought, tacky. The bright colors looked like just what they were—a hopeless attempt to brighten up a dreary place. A place where people came to die.

I was working myself up into my usual cheerful Sunshine Band mood.

I turned the corner and headed for the chapel with the whole group trailing along behind me. To my surprise, there were sounds of singing coming from the chapel. I opened the door a crack and looked in. The place was about half full, and kids in Pathfinder uniforms were standing in a row on the platform singing their little lungs out. I recognized a few of them from a nearby church.

Closing the door, I turned around to explain the situation to my group. The pleasant woman who'd met us at the door looked bewildered. "Oh,

I'm sure I knew you were coming," she said. "It's your regular week, isn't it—second Saturday of the month? Someone else must have arranged for this group to come without asking me. Oh, dear . . ." Her voice trailed off.

"Oh, well, these things happen," I said. I looked around at my sunshiners to see what we should do. I was hoping someone would suggest we just go home, but that didn't happen.

"I suppose we could just go in there and sit at the back and help sing," one of the girls suggested. The idea sounded good to me. I wouldn't have to get up front at all.

But the others didn't agree. "There must be all kinds of people who didn't come to the chapel," said Jeannie. She was the girl I'd asked to lead song service. "Maybe we could go around to the rooms and sing to them. You know, we could sort of walk up and down the halls singing."

Everyone seemed to like this suggestion, so I turned to the confused-looking woman. She said it would be OK. I think she was relieved to have the problem out of her hands.

The only problem left, as we trailed down the hall behind Jeannie, was that I didn't like the idea too much. *After all,* I figured, *all the people who want to listen to a program are already in the chapel. The ones who are left in their rooms are the ones who didn't want to come, right? So how are they going to feel when we bring it right into the privacy of their rooms?* I lagged behind the others. Jeannie was definitely in charge now. Maybe I could just duck out the side entrance and never be missed.

A little while later, as we swung around a corner and into our third rendition of "Peace Like a River," I decided I'd better go into one of the rooms. This wasn't easy. When I go to the hospital to visit someone, I keep my eyes on the heels of the person in front of me so I won't have to look into any of the rooms. Nursing homes aren't much better than hospitals, and sometimes they're worse.

I stopped by one of the rooms and forced myself to put a foot inside. With crocheted afghans on both beds the room looked more homey than most of the others I'd seen.

"Come in, dear. That's beautiful music you're playing out there."

What a relief! "I'm glad you like it," I said.

The first things that caught my eye, besides the two elderly women smiling at me, were the pictures on the wall. They were old pictures, brownish, but they looked as sharp as if they'd been taken last week. The one in front of me was of a woman holding a child. "Is this you?" I asked hesitantly, pointing to the mother.

"Oh, no, no," the woman replied. She was the same one who'd asked me to come in. "That's my husband with his mother. Taken when he was 5 years old."

"Wow." I tried to guess how long ago the picture must have been taken. Around the turn of the century, anyway. I looked at the next one. It was of a young man in a uniform.

"That was my husband in World War I," the woman explained.

"Wow." I realized my comments were getting a little repetitious, but I couldn't help it.

I stuck my head out into the corridor. "Jerry, come here for a second. There's something I want you to see." Photography was Jerry's hobby, and I knew he'd be interested. He came in, and Mrs. Tanner (I'd just read her name on the door) told him about the old pictures as I wandered around the room, looking at the rest of them. There was one on the dresser of a whole group of young men in uniform. "My husband with his regiment," Mrs. Tanner explained. "It was taken the same time as the one on the wall."

I scanned the rows of young faces, trying to figure out which was the late Mr. Tanner. Usually the faces in old pictures looked all the same to me, but I did manage to identify my host's husband. She seemed pleased that I'd been able to spot him.

"We were married right after the war," Mrs. Tanner told me.

"Wow, really?" I sat down on the edge of the bed near her rocking chair and listened to her stories about her husband and the war. Jerry was still wandering around looking at the pictures. Every so often he'd interrupt to ask Mrs. Tanner something about them. He kept saying "Wow" too. I figured that since he knew so much about photography, his "Wow" was more educated than mine had been. I was enjoying just listening to Mrs. Tanner and her roommate, Mrs. Drover.

Jerry finally pulled me away. We couldn't hear singing in the hall anymore. "We'd better go catch up with the others. Thanks for showing us the pictures, Mrs. Tanner. They're really something."

I said goodbye to the two women, and they said goodbye to us. Then Jerry and I hurried down the hall to find the rest of the group. Jerry was saying something technical about how you could preserve old photos in that kind of condition for so many years. I didn't understand, and I was only half listening. All I knew was that the two old women and their photographs had made me feel happy and lighthearted and just a little crazy. I skipped down the quiet hall ahead of Jerry.

We finally found the others, just finishing up. We sang the last two songs with them, then said goodbye to the people in the rooms around us. The Pathfinders had finished by the time we passed the chapel. I thanked Jeannie for taking charge of things, and she said she'd really enjoyed it.

As we left the lobby, I pulled on my raincoat and picked up one of the stacks of songbooks. We hadn't used them at all. I found when I got outside that I wasn't going to need the raincoat, either. The rain had stopped, and the sun was shining weakly through a tiny blue rift in the clouds.

It was nice, the sunshine, but it didn't really matter. After all, the sunshine was inside.

18
The Fastest Bug
by Jan S. Doward

The excitement around Jim's neighborhood was growing into a fevered pitch. Every boy between the ages of 10 and 15 was making a soapbox "bug," or go-cart, for the races down the big hill to Puget Sound. Each bug would move solely by gravity.

Jim worked away with John and Harold, determined to make the "bug of all bugs." They wanted a rocket-shaped racer that would roll faster than anything on wheels. They pounded and hammered, oiled bearings and sawed. Gradually the Rocket—the name they gave it—took shape. Jim realized it would have been nearly impossible without the help of Harold, who was older and more mechanical. John was rather slow with tools but gave good moral support. Jim worked fast but made so many mistakes that Harold insisted he go away sometimes.

"You fumblers stay your distance while I get these wheels adjusted," commanded Harold.

Jim and John stepped back. Their feelings ordinarily would have been hurt. But with the important job at hand, they let such comments slide.

"Harold knows his stuff, all right," nodded John.

Jim grunted his approval.

Harold rose and stood back to look at the Rocket. "She's a fine one," he muttered to himself.

"Do you think," Jim asked expectantly, "that she'll outrace Wally Parkhurst's bug?"

"Naturally," Harold boasted. "You don't think I'd build anything that'd come in second, do you?"

This satisfied both Jim and John. Now they just had to get the Rocket on the road and try it out. Jim was delegated to be chief driver, as he was the smallest and could fit into the cockpit the best. This delighted Jim, and he swelled with pride.

"Hold it steady to the center now while John and I give a big push," instructed Harold.

After a mighty heave, the Rocket shot down the gentle slope in front of Jim's house. To be sure, it rolled better than any bug yet to appear in the neighborhood. Now to try it down the steep hill on 132nd Street. The boys took turns riding the Rocket on the gradual incline to the big hill. Stopping at the top, they rested and talked over plans for racing.

"This is the best hill in the country," John announced as he looked down the long, twisting road ahead.

"Not only the best, but the steepest by far," added Jim. "Just wait until I take it around the banked corner near the bottom. I'll be doin' 80!"

Jim tried the hill first, with John and Harold running as fast as they could behind to watch him take the corners. Before the evening was over, every boy had had several chances to prove his driving ability. And they all felt sure that no one had a racer as fast as the Rocket.

Jim began to brag to the other children gathering at the hill to watch. Of course, Harold and John needed no encouragement in boasting either, and it was soon known by all within three blocks that the Rocket was the best. It so happened that there was not another racing bug around to prove the point at the time.

The next afternoon, however, brought several contenders to challenge the Rocket. Even Wally Parkhurst showed up with his sleek racer. It looked more like a factory-built job than any of the rest and always gave the Rocket a good run in every try down 132nd Street. Nevertheless Jim, Harold, and John felt confident they could finish far ahead, even if their bug had lost a few times. After several trial runs they prepared for the big race.

"All set?" called Jim from his cockpit.

"All set," chorused Harold and John.

The boys pushing Wally's bug to the white chalk mark nodded too. Their own private rules permitted a big push to a designated line, and then the bugs were to roll free.

"Ready . . . Go!"

The two bugs looked even as they started out, but gradually the Rocket moved ahead. Faster and faster they went. Now they were nearing the first turn. Swish around the corner and down the steep second grade. This was the hill, all right! The Rocket was at least one length in front now. The final banked corner came up fast. Jim leaned hard to the left, and the Rocket shot ahead to finish by a good two and a half lengths.

Jim burst with pride as he stepped out of the cockpit. Wally looked rather crestfallen. If Jim had been any kind of sport, he would have complimented his opponent on a good race. Instead, he let out a barrage of boasting and ridicule that made Wally pull his bug slowly up the hill without saying a word. It was hard to lose. But it was certainly harder for Jim to win. Poor sportsmanship never makes for fun or friends, but Jim and his companions had never learned this.

"Who won?" shouted Harold as he ran breathlessly around the corner to meet Jim coming back up.

"I did, of course. We have the best racing bug, and I'm the best driver."

When they reached the top of the hill, all the spectators heard their loud boasting. Wally turned to go home, but Jim threw a challenge that stopped him dead in his tracks.

"I'll tell you what, Wally Parkhurst," smirked Jim haughtily. "All three of us'll ride the Rocket and still beat you to the last corner."

"Take him up on it," someone shouted.

Others chorused their approval. This really would be a race with a capital R.

Wally agreed, and the three got their heads together and consulted about the seating arrangement. Everybody laughed as Harold straddled the hood and John sat atop the sloping back end.

"What you fellows need is a covered wagon," laughed Wally,

"You just wait until we finish first, and then make your smart remarks," shouted Jim.

The bragging about the famous Rocket continued, even after the race got under way. Harold kept calling names to Wally as the two bugs rushed toward the steepest part. John, however, had no time for anything but keeping his perch. He was definitely receiving some brutal treatment with the constant bouncing. But he somehow managed to stay on, even around corners.

"I should have brought—ouch!—a pillow," he screamed in Jim's ear.

Jim was too busy to answer, but he could well imagine John's crisis. Whatever had made him make a challenge like this, anyway? He could barely see the road, with Harold's big head in the way. And it was twice as hard to hold the steering wheel steady with so much weight. The Rocket was doing more weaving than anything else.

Several times Jim barely missed colliding with Wally's bug in their mad dash downhill. The two bugs were approaching the last banked corner now, with Wally far in the lead. Jim began leaning to the left as usual, but Harold was counteracting this movement altogether. And poor John—well, John's movements were more on the up-and-down order. Jim pulled hard to the left, but the great Rocket zigged when it should have zagged. It headed straight for the opposite side.

"Hang on; we're goin' into the brush!" shrieked Jim.

Harold didn't need any information about that. He could well see the nettles and thornbushes at the side of the road. It was happening so fast that none of the boys realized the real danger. For right at the side of the road, hidden by the thick foliage, was a deep drainage ditch. The Rocket, true to its name, careened into the brush and dropped out of sight. There was one huge crash, three loud screams, and that was all. The Rocket was no more.

Harold got scratched from head to toe. Jim's knees became terribly bruised from jamming them into the dashboard. And John received a good kink in his neck when he rammed his head into Jim's lap. But the boys also gained a lesson in pride that afternoon, having personally demonstrated the Bible truth that pride goes before a fall.

19
The Great Shoe Adventure
by Mary Louise Kitsen

David and Bruce frowned as they heard the announcement come over the speaker at the youth center. "The snowstorm predicted for tonight is coming early. Snow is expected to start falling any minute. The center will close immediately. Anyone unable to locate transportation home should report to the office."

"Oh, no," said Bruce. "I was really looking forward to shooting baskets."

"So was I," sighed David. "Guess we'll just have to do it another time."

The boys put on their coats and boots. An earlier storm had already dumped more than nine inches of snow on the ground. Winters could be pretty rough in Connecticut, and this winter seemed to be no exception.

"Come on," said Bruce. "We can catch the 2:15 bus if we hurry."

The first flakes began falling just as the bus arrived. The boys quickly boarded along with several other young people who'd been at the youth center.

Looking out the window, the boys were amazed at how fast the snow was building up. Still, the ride to their street was short, so they weren't worried. After all, the storm had just started.

The bus slid to a stop at the corner of Shelby and Marshall streets. The door opened, and two women climbed on board. One carried a bag of groceries. The other was shabbily dressed in a thin, crudely patched coat.

"Look at her feet," Bruce whispered to David.

David glanced down. "She doesn't have any shoes on!" he gasped. "Only a pair of heavy socks!" David furrowed his brow. *How can anyone walk in this weather without shoes?* he thought. *Won't her feet freeze? There must be something I can do to help. But what?*

"Anyone want off at Beecher or Tremont?" yelled the bus driver. "If not, I won't try those turns."

"We get off at Tremont, sir," said Bruce. "But we can get off at Beecher and walk the block and a half to our homes."

The bus slid as it stopped at Beecher. "You sure about this?" the bus driver called out. "I hate to see you kids walking in this weather. But with this storm, I'm worried about making my run as it is."

"We'll be fine," Bruce replied.

He got up, but David sat for a moment. Then he looked down at his boots. He was sure they'd be big enough.

"Come on, guys. I don't want to lose any more time," said the bus driver in a firm tone.

"I'm coming," said David. He leaned down and quickly untied his boots, then slipped them off. Quietly he handed them over to the stocking-footed woman who was sitting behind the driver.

The woman gasped. "But your feet! You can't—"

"I'll be fine," interrupted David as he headed out the door. "I've got another pair at home."

"God bless you. God bless you," the woman called after him as the door of the bus closed.

The snow was really dense now. "I've never seen it get so bad so fast," said David. The cold soaked through his socks, and his feet felt as though they were on fire. It was worse than he had expected.

"Are you all right?" asked Bruce. "We've got to keep moving."

David tried to run. "I didn't think my feet would hurt so bad."

Bruce stopped. "Listen, I'll take off one of my boots. We can each wear one and lean on each other and kind of hop." Bruce leaned against a fence and tried to untie his boot. Finally he slipped his mittens off.

"Here, now put this on," said Bruce as he handed David the boot. "Oh, no. Now I can't find my mittens. Well, it's too cold to spend much time looking. Let's just go."

The boys put their arms around each other and started hopping down the street. It was slow and difficult. But they made progress little by little.

"Ooh! My hands are really hurting," said Bruce.

"Hey, I can share my mittens like you shared your boot." David pulled off one mitten, and Bruce put it on. They started off again, with each boy having one hand in his jacket pocket.

The snow was coming down thicker and thicker. And the faster the snow fell, the slower the boys went.

"Do you think we'll make it?" asked Bruce.

"We'll make it," said David. But he wasn't as certain as he sounded.

Just then the boys heard a sound and saw a light shining through the falling snow.

"It's a snowplow," Bruce announced. "We've got to get to the side. The driver might not see us." In their hurry to get to the edge of the road, they slipped and fell. As they struggled to get up, the lights of the truck came closer and closer. Their hands and feet were so cold that they could hardly move.

Suddenly they heard the sound of brakes. The next thing they knew, strong arms reached down and picked them up. Minutes later they were inside a warm truck, making their way to the hospital.

"I don't think your hands or feet are frozen," said the truck driver, "but it's best to be certain. What were you doing out in this weather anyway, with only one pair of boots between you?"

"Well, you see, there was this woman on the bus," replied Bruce. And he related what David had done.

"So you gave your boots away, just like that." The truck driver cleared his throat. "You know, my wife and I are going to become parents for the first time next month. And, well, I just hope we have a couple of kids as great as you two."

David and Bruce looked at each other and smiled. The great shoe adventure was over. But the effects of it were just beginning.

20

The River
by Maylan Schurch

A long, long time ago (clap-clap),
As all you children know (clap-clap),
Uncle No-ah built himself an ARK!

The earliteen girls clap-clapped. Eight junior girls who should have been back in their own tent clap-clapped. Some of the earliteen boys clap-clapped. The earliteen leader, standing back by the rear door, clap-clapped. The song leader would have clap-clapped too if he hadn't been playing the guitar.

Matthew and I did not clap-clap. We sat stiffly, not singing, hoping that the meeting would soon be over, hoping that the Noah song would die away, hoping that the speaker would get up and say what he had to say and dismiss us out into the warm evening air.

For 40 days and nights (clap-clap),
The rain was sure a fright (clap-clap).

I made a decision. "Matthew," I whispered, "let's go."

He swiveled his head around at me and frowned.

I frowned back. "Matthew, I'm going. I've got to get out of here."

Matthew glanced nervously back over his shoulder at the earliteen leader, and then at his watch, and then at me. I knew he was worried about leaving, but since he was staying in my tent, he didn't feel as if he had much choice.

I slid away from him toward the aisle, and in 10 seconds I had reached the great outdoors, just beyond where the leader stood.

Matthew joined me, panting slightly. "What about your uncle?" he whispered.

"What about him?"

"What if he comes here looking for us?"

"He won't come," I said. "He doesn't want to miss any of the main meeting tonight. He just told me to be back at our tent by 10:00."

A sharp, enthusiastic *clap-clap* from the leader made us both jump.

"What are you going to do?" Matthew asked, lowering his voice.

"Let's go down to the river."

"Where?"

"The river."

Going down to the river wasn't easy. First, we had to stay out of sight of the security car that roamed the camp meeting grounds. We also had to keep a sharp eye out for my uncle, who held the earnest belief that all earliteen kids should go to all earliteen programs and who just might skip part of the main meeting after all.

Finally the coast was clear, and we squeezed under a chain-link fence and slid down a long bank to a rutted road. We followed this road until we came to a wheat field. Once across the field, we fought our way under a long, high hedge of blackberry bushes and clambered down another bank to the river.

The river wasn't all that great. If there'd been a shore, there might have been some skipping rocks. But there wasn't any shore. Just a lot of slippery, moss-covered rocks sticking up out of the water. We jumped around on these for a while, but that got old fast.

"Let's go to that 7-Eleven on the edge of town and get some Cheetos," I said. "I've got some cash."

When the last of our Cheetos was gone, we wandered over to a nearby roller skating rink and watched the skaters for a while. Eventually the rink closed, so we decided to head back.

"What time is it?" I asked Matthew.

He tilted his watch so a streetlight would shine on it.

"Eleven fifty-five. Your uncle is going to kill you."

"I doubt it." I crumpled my Cheetos sack and tossed it into a dumpster. "He probably figures we're just running around on the grounds."

It was about a mile to the campgrounds, so it was probably way past midnight when we got to the main gate. I was expecting to see a security person with a walkie-talkie, but the little gatehouse was dark and deserted.

"What are you going to say when we get in?" Matthew asked.

"Stop worrying," I said. "I'll think of something. Just make sure you back me up."

We turned in at our row of tents. The gritty crunch of gravel told us that a car was approaching along the lane we'd just left.

"Security," I said, and we dove between two tents, landing on our stomachs. Suddenly the row of tents was lit with a blue-white brilliant light.

Matthew hiccuped. "I didn't know the security car had a spotlight like that," he whispered. "I wonder what they're looking for."

"Us," I said, chuckling.

"You think so?"

"Of course not," I said scornfully. "I wish you'd stop being such a wimp, Matthew. Maybe a little kid's gotten lost or something."

Matthew was up on his knees, peering around the tent at the retreating car. "That's not security's car," he said. "It's the cops!"

I got up, rubbing my face where a tent rope had burned it as we'd dived for cover. "Something must be up. Let's go check it out."

We circled around and approached the security trailer from behind through a grove of trees. We saw two white cars labeled SHERIFF parked in front of it, plus the security car.

"Hold it," I said when we'd come within about 30 feet. We stood single file behind a thick tree with low branches. Two men stood outside the trailer. Something seemed funny about the way they were dressed. "They're wearing waders."

"I knew they were looking for us," Matthew said in a frightened, little kid's voice.

"They can't be. We didn't tell anybody we were going down to the river."

"Maybe somebody heard us in earliteens."

"They couldn't have," I insisted. "Everybody was singing 'Noah's Ark' and clapping."

"The leader must have heard us back at the door," Matthew said, panic in his voice. "There! See? He just came out of the trailer."

Sure enough, there was the earliteen leader. He walked over to where the two men in waders stood. And in the glare from the porch light I saw that his pants were slick and shiny and wet.

Matthew hiccuped again. He sounded as if he were going to be sick. I was just about to turn around and try to quiet him down when a movement caught my eye. Someone had come into the office, someone whose jacket was dark and stained. When his face came into the full light, I recognized my uncle. As I watched him, the spark of fear I'd felt melted away. His face was white, and his lips were pinched and scared. I'd never seen him like that. He bent down. I could tell he was dialing the phone. He blinked a couple times, then straightened up, waiting. I knew he was calling my parents.

"Matthew, come on," I said, watching my uncle.

"Where are you going?"

"Stay here if you want to. I'll be back to get you." I broke from the tree and ran toward the trailer window. I saw my uncle put a hand to his eyes and begin to speak. I reached the window and banged on it. My uncle glanced briefly at the window, but kept on talking. I banged again and waved wildly. Then he saw me.

Later the security chief, who had a bark that bit, raked us over the coals for 10 solid minutes. He told us how the earliteen leader had reported that he thought he'd overheard us say a word that sounded like river and how they'd followed our trail across the wheat field, had seen our shoe marks on the rocks, and had searched the river for a half mile in the dark, looking for our bodies.

The four cold-eyed deputy sheriffs who'd helped with the search swore at us for causing all that trouble, and then, remembering they were at a religious gathering, they begged everybody's pardon except ours.

And even though my uncle grounded us solidly for the rest of camp meeting, and even though we had to sit through 18 more performances of the Noah song, nothing really mattered as much as the tear-stained expression on my uncle's face when he looked through that security trailer window into my eyes, recognized me, and sobbed for joy.

21

Fakebite

by Randy Fishell

Drill sergeants and children share a unique characteristic. They demand a great deal of attention.

Following the lead of Gomer Pyle, I might have chosen a similar lifestyle as one of America's best. But the Marine Corps, exhibiting true military intelligence, forbids the enlistment of 9-year-old combatants. So instead I joined the ranks of attention-seeking children.

My limited experience had already shown that there were relatively few situations that lent themselves to the practice of undisguised self-centeredness. There was one occasion, however, that did provide an opportunity to help satisfy my need for others to notice me—the annual church picnic.

This year the picnic committee chose scenic Riverview Park as the perfect spot for an afternoon of fellowship and festivities. Here men, women, and children alike were afforded an unobstructed view of a complete chemical waste transportation system. (In earlier times this was called a river.) Any church picnicker who so desired could munch a bunch of Fritos while watching endless varieties of chemical waste drift lazily by.

Of course, we youngsters were unaffected by such adult concerns as environmental hazards. It wasn't long before most of us boys decided to cool off in the murky mess. Shortly the sounds of carefree summer delight filled the air.

"Watch out for this broken beer bottle over here."

"Hey, what's this brick doing in the water?"

"I just saw a snake!"

A snake! I didn't actually walk on water, but a couple seconds later I was standing on the bank. A group of concerned picnickers gathered around, and questions and commentary came rapid-fire from the crowd.

"How long was it?" Mr. Hoover asked.

"I'm not really sure," his son Mike reported, still trembling bravely in the water. "It was moving real fast!"

"I've heard there are water moccasins in this part of the river," another person chimed in.

I was no herpetologist, but I was pretty sure water moccasins weren't shoes especially designed for performing certain miraculous feats in a river.

Finally Mr. Hoover, apparently unconvinced of the threat of real danger, told Mike that if he saw the snake sneaking back into the area, he should just leave it alone. "It won't bite anybody unless you give it a reason to," he informed us all.

Snakebite, huh? My wheels of creativity churned into motion. It would make quite an impact on my friends and family if they thought I had actually been bitten by a snake. Especially a water moccasin.

Suddenly I envisioned Dad kneeling at the foot of my deathbed. His eyes full of sorrow, he repented and begged forgiveness for the myriad times he had unjustly administered the board of correction to me.

Mom would weep openly, admitting her wrongness in asking me to perform such unreasonable and slavish tasks as picking up my clothes. But still I would lie prone.

Then the door would gently open, and Jennifer Walker would enter. Between sobs, she'd speak. "If only I'd had a chance to tell him how much I cared," she'd lament. "I was even going to sit next to him on the bus tomorrow."

The plan was a go-ahead. But I would have to make it look good. Fortunately, my fertile mind had already conceived an idea.

Making my way toward the rear of the crowd, I slithered over to a nearby picnic table and sat down. A brief glance around confirmed that nobody had seen me. I closed my eyes and opened my mouth. In a remarkable display of senselessness, I proceeded to bite down on my right kneecap.

Based on the amount of pain I experienced, I knew that my immediate goal had been accomplished.

"*Yeoooww!*" I screeched, grabbing my indented knee.

All heads turned in my direction. Mom and Dad dropped their potato salad and came running. So far, so good.

Pulling up beside me, my father asked anxiously, "What's the matter with your leg, son?"

Too scrupulous to tell an out-and-out lie, I whimpered and pointed to the well-embedded tooth marks adorning my knobby kneecap. Then, in an honest attempt to lead Dad and the other onlookers down a path of gross deception, I spoke. "Well, I didn't actually see the snake," I groaned, "but . . ."

Mother's face turned a shade of reptilian green. "Martin!" she shrieked. "Our son's been bitten by a snake!"

Right on cue. Perhaps the task at hand was going to be easier than I had originally thought. Although I was reasonably certain Dad had bought the story hook and line, his face registered a small sinker of doubt. Eyes narrowed, he leaned in close and surveyed my wound.

"You know," he said, stroking his chin, "there's something not quite right about this bite."

I squirmed, sensing a potential crack developing in the foundation of my fabrication.

Then he added, "And I think I know what it is."

My little sweat glands began pumping big-time perspiration. Given the situation, I knew that silent prayer would be inappropriate. Perhaps Dad would see fit to make this our little secret.

But pointing to the mark on my knee, he went on. "It's the way these tooth marks are laid out," he explained to the whole world. His convicting gaze now rose to meet my guilt-ridden face. "As nearly as I can tell," Dad espoused, "if the 'snake' that bit you were to grin real big, he'd have a gap between his two front teeth that perfectly matches that of another snake in the grass I happen to know of."

Pausing for effect, he then finished by adding, "Need I say more?" (The rough translation of which is "Your goose has been cooked.") His examination finished, Dad stood upright and crossed his arms in confident triumph.

I looked over at Mom, back at Dad, then down at the bite. How could I have overlooked such an obvious thing? In my haste to fake the snake, I had neglected to take into consideration the fact that I had inherited my grandpa Covault's irregular incisors. My two front teeth made Bugs Bunny's grinders look like dental perfection. For the first time in my adolescent experience, I wished I'd spent more time in the dentist's chair. But alas, that was all fluoride under the bridge now.

Lifting my head, I looked up at Dad. An angelic, lip-parting smile crossed my face. Perhaps this heartrending look of innocence would call forth a sympathetic response. Only too late did I realize that my beaming countenance merely revealed the crowning evidence of my guilt.

I haven't been back to Riverview Park for quite a while now. But its memory will linger on in my nightmares for years to come. As for my father, I eventually forgave him for his role in bringing my counterfeit bite to light. Jennifer Walker, on the other hand, probably married someone more secure than I. (And undoubtedly less exciting.)

All told, I did manage to glean a kernel of truth from my otherwise regrettable experience. Of course, had I been a little more shrewd, I might have already discovered that "the wisdom of the prudent is to give thought to their ways, but the folly of fools is deception" (Proverbs 14:8).

In other words, there are some things in life you just shouldn't sink your teeth into. They can cause you too much 'tention.

22
Body Odor, Hairy Legs, and Stinkin' Skis
by Karl Haffner

"John Jacob Jingleheimer Schmidt, that's my name too. Whenever I . . ." My mind drifted away from the chorus of campers as the bus rumbled down the Blue Ridge Parkway.

Why can't I get excited about ski camp like everyone else? I wondered. I was about as enthused as a mail carrier at a pit bull dog show.

"Da da da da da da da!" The kids bellowed the ending, half singing and half screaming. When the giggles subsided, they struck up the chorus again. "John Jacob Jingleheimer Schmidt . . ."

I glanced around the bus, noticing the empty seats. There were only two. The front seat next to Captain Menhart was vacant. But that was to be expected—every camper knew it was uncool to sit with the camp director. And then the seat next to me. Even the oaf two seats behind me (who looked like ET on steroids) at least had a friend to sit with.

"Da, da da da da da da! John Jacob Jingleheimer . . ."

The bus turned onto a gravel road winding through the Virginia forest. Occasionally we'd catch an enticing peek of the shimmering waters of Smith Mountain Lake. Of course, I was the only kid who was noticing any scenery.

"Da da da da da da da!"

The bus roared into Hickory Cove Camp about the same time the song had matured to just the last line and a chorus of giggles.

"OK, listen up!" Captain Menhart barked. "Welcome to camp. Get your stuff and get settled into your rooms. No one is to go to the waterfront until after lunch. Girls, remember: You are not allowed to wear bikinis, and you—"

"What if that's all we have?" interrupted the girl in the back seat with Elvira earrings and the personality of a truck stop.

"If that's all you brought, then you have to wear a T-shirt over it. And another thing: No fireworks. Is that understood?"

The kids grumbled a bit as Captain Menhart growled on. "And one final rule. Everyone must follow this rule. If you don't observe this rule, you're in hot water. The last and most important rule is: Have fun!"

The kids erupted in cheers as we scurried off the bus and into the lodge. The guys settled into the dank, open basement, while the girls invaded the private and cushy rooms on the first floor.

I tossed my orange sleeping bag on the last open bed. "Hey!" I exclaimed to no one in particular. "Why are there ants all over my bed?"

"Chuckie's food drove them out of the kitchen," the kid who'd claimed the bunk above me answered. "Hi, I'm Mike." He interrupted his unpacking long enough to shake my hand.

"I'm Karl."

"You been to Hickory Cove before?"

"No."

"It's not bad as long as you don't depend on Chuckie's food to keep you alive," he quipped, tossing me a Snickers bar.

"Thanks, uh, Mike. I guess you've been here before?"

"Yep. Well, I came last summer, for half a week, anyway. They sent me home after I painted Captain Menhart's dog purple. 'Old Meany Menhart' didn't see the humor in it. But this year I hope I can stick around long enough to learn to slalom—if the food here doesn't kill me first."

"You're a good water-skier, eh?"

"Yeah, pretty good," he boasted as he tossed his duffel bag on the bed. "Listen, I got to meet my buddies at the cafeteria. I'll see you around, OK?"

"Yeah, ah, good meeting you," I replied when he was almost out the door.

I glanced down. I gasped. I didn't want to believe my eyes—or my armpits! Sweat spots the size of Madagascar discolored my T-shirt.

I remembered a recent evening when Dad had bought me my first can of deodorant. He said the time had come when I was no longer a boy but a man. "Your body's going through a lot of changes," he told me. And even though I pooh-poohed Dad at the time, I was suddenly thankful for his insight.

Stripping off my smelly T-shirt, I reached for Dad's gift—a 32-ounce jumbo can of Right Guard. He even cared enough to send the "new and improved formula." I sprayed like a loaded crop duster.

"Hey, you doorknob!" protested a pudgy kid in the corner. "Don't spray so much! What are you trying to do? Gag us all?"

No, just you, I thought darkly. I could feel a burning blush melting onto my face. "Sorry," I replied sheepishly.

Things didn't start out much better in the afternoon. I splashed around in the water, waiting to ski and noticing the legs of all the other kids. Feeling self-conscious and embarrassed about my hairy legs, I stayed in the water as much as possible to conceal my turbo growth hormones. There was only one other camper who had legs as hairy as mine—but I hardly wanted to be classed with Esther "The Gorilla" Wolvertine.

I figured it was another one of those "body changes" Dad warned me about. I just couldn't figure out why my body (and Esther's) was changing so much faster and weirder than the other normal kids.

Two and a half hours later my number was finally called. "Number 28, your turn!" the ski boat driver shouted.

"That's me," I replied.

"Have you ever skied before?"

"No."

"Do you know what to do?"

"No."

"OK, listen; it's easy if you do what I say. Keep your arms straight, bend your knees, let the boat pull you up, and keep your skis straight. Got it?"

"Got it," I lied.

The Ski Nautique drifted forward, pulling the slack out of the rope. "Tell me when," the sunbaked driver instructed.

The instant my skis became untangled and the rope was between them, I hollered, "Hit it!"

Rrrrrrrrrrrrrr, the 351 engine roared. My left ski headed east while my right ski headed west. Soon I was buried in water.

"You've got to keep your skis straight," the driver snapped when he circled around to bring me the rope. "And put your knees next to your chest so there's not so much drag."

"I'll bet the drag is caused by the hair on my legs," I mumbled. After a five-minute battle to retrieve the skis and wrestle them on, I tried again. "Hit it!" Once again I collapsed and plunged beneath the water.

This ritual—klutz puts on skis, klutz tries to ski, klutz fails to ski, driver gets impatient with klutz—continued for 30 minutes. Finally, however, I earned the right to run to headquarters and call home.

"Hi, Dad."

"Well, hello! How's my favorite water-skier?" Dad's familiar voice was a welcome sound.

"Oh, pretty good. Guess what?"

"You need money."

"Yeah, now that you mention it. But guess what else?"

"What's that?"

"I got up on skis! I water-skied!"

"That-a-boy! I knew you could do it. That's terrific!"

"I dunno; most kids got it in three or four tries."

"At least you stuck with it until you learned," Dad encouraged.

"Yeah, I guess so."

"Well," Dad continued, "you've grown four inches in the past year. Your body is changing. Hang in there; coordination will come."

Later that evening Mike asked me if I wanted to go to campfire with him. "I've even got a couple live spiders to toss at the girls in case the program gets boring," he assured me.

We filed into our seats at the campfire bowl. A huge banner hanging from the front displayed the theme "God Made You Special!"

"Good evening," a young man welcomed us. "I'm Loren Kline, your program director. This week we'll be talking about how God has made each of us special and unique. To start out, turn to the person next to you and tell them how you think God has made them special. Take 30 seconds and do it now."

I turned to Mike and said, "I think God made you with a good sense of humor."

"Thanks," Mike replied. "I think God made you special by ah, um, giving you a low voice."

It wasn't that my voice was low; it just happened that my voice was changing—like the rest of my body—at an earlier age than most kids.

"OK, gang," Loren quieted the murmur, "now that you've had a chance to affirm the person next to you, I want to tell you a story of how I discovered that God made me special. It happened growing up on a farm in Rosebud, Texas. I was only 6 years . . ."

Just above his red hair, the words of the banner "God Made You Special!" echoed in my mind. Suddenly the untruth of the message hit me. It wasn't so much that God had made me special, like the banner advertised, but rather that God was still making me special.

23
Dangerous Dewey
by Jack Calkins

My dad spent most of his time in the Maryland State Penitentiary. He even got me in once or twice. Being the chief psychologist in a maximum-security prison meant he got to analyze some pretty heavy dudes.

My childhood was filled with stories about prison riots, hunger strikes, padded cells—and executions. I don't recommend that kind of childhood for everybody, but the Lord taught me some incredible things through my dad.

One prisoner my father tried hard to help was a guy named Dewey.* He'd been convicted of armed robbery and attended one of my dad's psychotherapy groups.

Dewey learned to trust Doc, as the prisoners called my dad. He was one of the few people Dewey would ever trust in his life.

I was about 10 years old when Dewey escaped. Everyone was looking for him. The governor even called out the Army to help. Being considered armed and dangerous, Dewey became the most wanted man in the state of Maryland. FBI staff and state and local police combed the streets of Baltimore looking for dangerous Dewey. But nobody could find him, and there was only one man Dewey would ever surrender to.

The black telephone in the dining room rang just after sundown. It was getting dark, and a storm had blown in. Mom answered and motioned for Dad to come take the call.

What I remember of the conversation went something like this: "Where are you? Don't move. I should be there in about 25 minutes. OK." Dad walked over to the closet at the bottom of the stairs, pulled out a thin khaki raincoat, and while buttoning it up (and without raising his eyes), said, "If I'm not back in one hour, call the police." As he opened the door, the wind blew in a sheet of rain. Dad slammed the door tight behind him.

We lived in a row house in northeast Baltimore, in a neighborhood of mostly brick houses with cement porches and sidewalks. The lightning lit up the slate roofs as the thunder bounced endlessly from one side of the street to the other, the kind of stuff movie sets try to copy.

My mom majored in cool. She was used to craziness, but this was something else.

"What're you gonna do, Mom?" I asked.

"Wait." She smiled back.

But how long? A half hour went by. The storm got real mean outside. Even the light from the streetlamp couldn't dent the darkness. I pressed my face against our front window. The pane was cold, and I wondered if Dad was.

When the hour was almost over, I whined, "When you gonna call, Mom?"

She crocheted another row, pushed her glasses back up on her nose, and sighed, "Not yet."

Another 15 minutes. "Now, Mom?"

"Let's just give him a few more minutes, honey."

My nerves were fried!

An hour and 25 minutes after Dad had pulled away into the blackness, he returned. I moved to the front window and watched two glistening figures come toward the house. Dad had him.

He pushed Dewey in the front door like some stray cat that didn't know how to accept hospitality. Dewey plastered himself up against the wall behind the door. He looked . . . scared! My 10-year-old mind said, *Scared?* The most wanted man in the state was standing, shaking, dripping water on our living room floor.

"This is the nicest house I've ever been in, ma'am," he softly choked to my mother.

"Take Mr. Dewey upstairs and get him shaved and showered, Jack," Dad said as he tossed his hat on the banister and stroked my head.

Sure, why not? I thought to myself as I got my first whiff of Dewey. *Boy, he must have hidden the past 14 nights in a trash can!*

He had.

Dewey was soaked to the skin. Old tobacco stench, booze, and garbage odor wafted from our little white-tiled bathroom. As I handed Mr. Dewey my dad's Gillette razor and shaving cream, it occurred to me how uncertain this whole situation was.

After a silent shower, he emerged from the steam-filled cavern. Mr. Dewey was transformed. His gaunt frame made a valiant effort to fill Dad's baggy pants. Then we went down the stairs and through the living room and made our entrance into the dining room. Mom had fixed some burgers and fries. Dewey smiled sheepishly and sat down as Mom scooted his chair toward the plate.

I distinctly remember the ketchup dripping down the corner of Dewey's mouth onto the napkin he'd tucked into my dad's flannel shirt. That moment will remain with me forever. There he sat, peaceful, contented, under control, *and* the most wanted man in Maryland. Well, Maryland would have to wait, 'cause dessert was next.

Suddenly the front door smashed open as if the lock hadn't existed! I'd never seen a real machine gun before. Especially one pointed in my general vicinity. It looked heavier than I'd imagined.

One of our neighbors had seen our car pull up and recognized Dewey. They didn't know if we were in danger or not, so they called the cops. And here the cops stood, dripping on the same spot Dewey had.

"Get your hands up!" the sergeant shouted at the criminal.

Dewey wiped the vanilla ice cream off his lips as he pushed the chair back and stood up. His face looked petrified. Now he was dangerous. I felt afraid for the first time since Dad had returned.

It was standard operating procedure for any suspect to be frisked immediately. Everything happened so fast, though, that the police forgot. But Dewey didn't. He was handcuffed, and as the officers escorted him through our lockless front door, he quickly leaned over and pulled an 8-inch shiv (that's a homemade knife) from his boot. Holding it by the blade, he handed it to my father while sneering at the sergeant.

Mr. Dewey could have carved us up. But his faith in my father tamed him. The most wanted man in the state had held my hand, let me lead him around like a puppy, and even apologized to me for the way he smelled. Kindness is sure powerful stuff.

Later in life, God's loving-kindness tamed me. Memories of ol' Dewey helped me appreciate the faithfulness of my heavenly Father's love. Whenever I'm tempted to wallow in self-righteous religion, I remember that crazy night, and that it was my father's faithfulness that had made all the difference.

It still does.

*I've changed the name to protect the guilty.

24

High-speed Hunt

by Charles Mills

Larry squinted down the long rifle barrel and waited. The metal sighting tab mounted on the far end of the weapon moved rhythmically in response to his beating heart. The boy knew he'd simply fire between beats. Anyone who hunted jackrabbits in Kansas understood that old trick.

Slowly his index finger squeezed the trigger. Crack! The aging .22 sent a tiny projectile slicing over the wheat field. Larry saw the bullet slam into the ground inches from a rabbit's foot. The animal jumped straight up into the air, turned, and came down running.

The boy moaned. "Missed," he said to his cousin Wendel, who was sprawled on the warm earth beside him.

"We're going about this all wrong," Wendel stated, removing the thin wheat stalk from his lips and waving it in the air. "I mean, here we are, a couple of top-notch small-game hunters, and the state of Kansas is offering 10 cents for each jackrabbit we bring down. More for coyotes, badgers, and skunks. And we're sitting here hoping some animal is dumb enough to amble into our line of fire."

"So?"

"So we need to increase our line of fire."

"How?"

Wendel shook his head and chuckled. "Do I need to explain everything to you? I think it's time we take this show on the road." The speaker moved closer to his cousin. "Look, your dad likes to buy and sell stuff, like old cars. He's got a four-door Model T sitting behind your barn even as we speak, right?"

"Right."

"And my brother owns a .410-gauge shotgun with lots of ammo hidden away at my place, right?"

A mischievous grin creased Larry's 12-year-old face. "What if we're caught?"

"Who's going to know? Everyone who'd get in our way has gone to town. We've got the whole afternoon to pull this thing off."

They stumbled to their feet and hurried to the nearby farm. Soon they were speeding down a dusty road leading away from cousin Wendel's place, with Larry's younger brother Mike seated between them in the vibrating, rattling, topless Model T Ford. This operation would need three skilled participants: one to drive, one to spot, one to fire.

It had been decided that Mike, the youngest member of the team, was the best aim when it came to bagging jackrabbits. Larry would sit behind the wheel of the jostling vehicle while sharp-eyed Wendel would search the horizon for the telltale silhouette of two pointy ears sticking up into the blue Kansas sky.

They traveled two miles across the flatland to a pasture where a herd of grazing cattle moved slowly in the midday sun. Sure enough, just as they went through the cattle gate, Wendel eagerly pointed to the west. Mike nodded, slipped a big shell into the gun, stood, aimed, and fired. *Blam!* The grass beside the jackrabbit disintegrated, leaving the animal exposed. But before the boy could get off the second shot, the quick-footed creature was gone. The cattle ran in all directions, frightened by the powerful report of the rifle.

"There!" Wendel whispered. Larry turned the bouncing car to the left as Mike pulled back on the hammer and squeezed the trigger.

Blam! A nearby bush exploded as shot broke it into mulch.

"Over there!" the spotter called excitedly. Larry turned the steering wheel as Mike jammed the gun against his shoulder.

Blam! Nothing moved on the ground as the shell's contents simply vanished over the horizon.

This went on time and time again as the warm, lazy sun moved through the deep-blue sky.

At last the hunters came upon a barbed-wire fence. They stopped the Model T and cut the wires, for just on the other side of a distant swell in the ground Wendel was sure he saw a couple of promising targets.

But try as they might, they couldn't make a hit. Something was wrong with their great scheme, and each had his own opinion as to why their afternoon wasn't going as planned.

Finally it was decided that hunting jackrabbits with a shotgun from a bouncing Model T Ford just might not be such an outstanding idea after all. The boys drove home in the gathering shadows of evening, dejected, disappointed, and hungry.

Early the next morning, while Larry and his family were eating, a firm knock sounded at the back door of their farmhouse. Wendel's father stood just beyond the screen, a strong hand gripping his son's shoulder.

"We've got problems," he reported. "Big problems."

Larry and Mike sank down in their chairs. They knew that somehow their little escapade had come to light.

"I'll take care of my sons," they heard their father say after a hushed conversation at the back door, "and you take care of yours."

It seemed that Wendel's brother had discovered that his supply of shotgun shells had been greatly reduced. And a neighbor had discovered that someone had cut his fence, allowing his cattle to wander away. Others in the area had reported seeing a group of young boys driving across pastureland shooting at anything that moved—a very dangerous activity, even for Kansas.

For the next few days Larry and Mike found it more convenient to stand for meals than sit. And to add insult to injury, they were required to work even beyond their daily chore list: feeding and milking the cows, caring for the farm's horses, looking after the chickens, harnessing the work animals, cutting the grass in the big yard, repairing miles of fences—labors that began at 4:30 in the morning and didn't end until 10:00 at night.

For they had to find ways to earn enough cash to repay their father, who'd made good with the neighbors so they could repair their fences and get herds of cattle sorted out and in the right pastures again. There was also the matter of replacing boxes of expensive shotgun shells stolen from Wendel's brother.

"At first I didn't think our punishment fit the crime," Larry will tell you today. "Farm life in 1926 was flat-out hard. But as the years rolled by, I began to see the foolishness of our actions. Not only did we drive a car we shouldn't have been driving, through pastures we had no business in, with a shotgun that could have killed a cow—or one of us—very easily, but we also put our neighbors in very real danger. That old Model T jumped around like a rabbit itself. A shot from a .410-gauge weapon can travel a long, long way. We had no idea what or who was just beyond our line of sight."

There's something else Larry learned from the experience. Strangely enough, it has to do with God. "Sometimes we may not appreciate our heavenly Father's rules and regulations. We think He's being too harsh on us. But when we look back, we see the foolishness of our actions and discover that obedience to His laws was really a good idea after all."

Larry, Mike, and Wendel will never forget their high-speed hunt. Whenever they see a jackrabbit popping up out of a Kansas field, they think of that day in the Model T and smile. For it was during those years they began to learn about responsibility—and about God.

25
My Nasty Victory
by Jane Chase

I knew it. Picked last again. Out of a gym class of 48, my friend Mary and I were the only ones left to be chosen for wall ball teams. OK, I guess technically I wasn't last, since I got picked before Mary, but it felt like last. *Good ol' Jane and Mary,* I thought. *Always last.*

The two teams lined up against the walls on opposite sides of the gym. In wall ball, people on one team try to throw large rubber balls between the people on the other team and hit the wall. Each clean hit is worth one point. But if someone catches the ball as it bounces off the wall—before it hits the floor or another player—the point doesn't count.

Mr. Wright, our gym teacher (who says he can never be wrong because he is always "Wright"), tossed a ball toward our team, the red team. Of course, John caught it. He's one of the best athletes in our class. He passed to his best friend, Mark, who passed to another guy. The red team was spread out all over our half of the gym, passing back and forth, jockeying for position, looking for a good opportunity to whip the ball through the blue team and hit their wall.

Most of the action was going on in the center of the floor, so I hung off to one side, where I knew no one was likely to throw the ball. I pretended I was playing so I wouldn't look like a total loser. I'd trot a few steps forward, a few steps back, shuffle-step to the side a bit, and wave my arms, as if I were positioning myself for a good throw and signaling for the ball.

A few seconds later Mr. Wright tossed a second ball to the blue team. Now I had to pretend I was defending the red team's wall as well as ready to go on the offense. Then Mr. Wright tossed in another two balls.

Balls flew everywhere, hitting the walls and bouncing off players. I just kept doing my dance along the edge of the floor, praying a ball wouldn't come my way.

Just then I noticed Mary, who was opposite me on the blue team, doing the same thing. She hung near the edge of the floor, moving around a bit, but not really playing. No one else was near her, since they wanted to be where the action was.

No problem, I thought. *The two of us can just bide our time until the end of the period.* Being picked last for teams made us look bad enough—we didn't have to make it worse by actually playing.

Then the unthinkable happened. A ball came toward me! I knew I would look really stupid if I just stepped aside, so I grabbed it.

"Hey, over here!" John yelled. He stood at front center, poised to catch my pass and whip it over into blue territory.

Instead, I glanced at Mary. She still stood alone at the edge of the floor. Instead of passing to John, I threw the ball as hard as I could at her. For an instant she looked shocked, then dodged the hard-thrown missile. The ball bounced off the wall behind her and hit the floor before anyone could catch it.

I'd made a point for our team!

I could hardly believe it, but it sure felt good. Then I saw John looking at me, surprise on his face. I grinned, and he nodded. The next time someone passed him a ball, he passed it to me, and I whipped it at Mary again. Another point!

For the rest of the game John kept passing to me, and I kept scoring. Oh, I felt kind of sorry for Mary—after all, she was my friend, and I was making her look bad. But my technique was working, and it felt too good to stop.

By the end of the period our red team had way outscored the blue. When Mr. Wright blew the whistle signaling the end of PE class, I trotted happily toward the girls' locker room. I strutted in, grinning, waiting for the congratulations. But as I snapped open my locker, I heard someone say, "Ball hog."

I turned and saw Jody, who was usually the star of the team, glaring at me. *She's just jealous,* I thought. *Today I won the game, not her.*

"Yeah," Carolyn spoke up. "In wall ball you're supposed to pass the ball, not just throw it at the other team the first chance you get."

"Well, we won, didn't we?" I challenged. "Isn't that what matters?"

Angry that I hadn't received the praise I deserved, I changed clothes quickly and slammed my locker closed. As I left the room, I saw Mary, off to one side as usual, looking sullen. But I didn't worry about it. After all, we were friends; she'd get over it. I knew she'd understand that I couldn't pass up the opportunity to be the star just once. And if it came at her expense, oh well.

As I walked through the gym on my way out, I saw Mr. Wright rolling away the rack of rubber balls. "Nice scoring, Jane," he said.

I felt the warmth of success wash over me. "Thanks." *See,* I soothed my troubled conscience. *And Mr. Wright is always right.*

Later, in study hall, as usual I sat next to Mary. I pulled my desk over to hers so we could work on math problems together. I enjoyed last-period study hall, because Ms. Kantar let us talk, as long as we kept it low.

"I started doing the problems on page 57," I whispered to Mary, "but I got stuck on number 9. What did you get?"

Mary didn't answer. She had her math book out too, but didn't even look at me.

"What's the matter?" I asked. "Are you still mad about gym class? I was only trying to help my team win."

Mary looked up, and I saw the hurt in her eyes. "Winning is one thing," she said softly, "but did you have to humiliate me to do it?"

"I didn't mean to humiliate you," I retorted. "I mean, everyone already knows you're not good in sports. I'm not either. That's why I had to do it."

"You didn't have to. I saw you over on the side, pretending to be interested in the game, but secretly hoping you wouldn't have to play. What if someone had purposely kept shooting balls at you, knowing you'd miss?" She looked down at her book and curled the edge of the page under her thumb. "I would never do that to you," she whispered.

That's when I realized Mary was right, and Mr. Wright was wrong. He'd called it "nice scoring," but it wasn't nice at all. It had been mean and cruel. I'd followed the rules of the game, but I hadn't been following God's rule—the golden rule. Somehow I knew God wouldn't coach me to win at all costs.

"I'm sorry, Mary. Those few minutes of stardom weren't worth it." I smiled sheepishly. "Especially when everyone else in the locker room was mad at me too." I paused. "I hope you'll forgive me."

Mary smiled. "OK. Besides," she added playfully, "they'll probably never throw you the ball again anyway."

"Hey!" I said, pretending to be angry.

"Score one for me, huh? Just kidding."

Somehow I knew our friendship would survive.

26
Promises, Promises
by Carolyn Rathbun

I'd always wanted a cat of my own, but the landlord of our Pennsylvania apartment didn't allow pets, so I'd never had one. The fact that Jason, my new stepdad, had a cat was the only good thing about "the big move."

"We can't afford to keep two houses," my mom had explained after the wedding.

"I've put my ranch up for sale," Jason chimed in, "but your mother and I have agreed that if it doesn't sell, we'll move in together as a family."

Well, the ranch didn't sell, and we were headed west. "When we get to our home," Jason had told me, "Billy Bob, my overgrown kitten, will be all yours. I promise."

"You'll love Montana!" my best friend, Sherae, had sniffled the morning we moved. "Maybe I can come visit. Anyhow, write and send pictures of your new cat, OK?"

Unable to speak through the lump in my throat, I hugged my best friend a final time before a huge sob escaped my lips. Mom helped me—and the giant stuffed panda Sherae had given me—into the back seat of Jason's long pickup cab. Out the back window I watched the U-Haul trailer—with all Mom's and my earthly goods—bounce along behind us.

The past four years had been a blur. After Dad left us, Mom about killed herself holding down two jobs to put food on our table and keep me in a Christian school. Dad would call and say something like he was sending a Christmas present or coming to be with me on my birthday. He always ended these phone visits with "I promise." But guess what? It never seemed to happen. So I finally just gave up on him—and on God. *Don't trust anyone who makes promises,* I told myself. *Then maybe you won't get hurt anymore.*

I didn't say much as Jason's pickup truck ticked off the miles between my old life and the new. One worrisome thought, though, kept racing around in my head like an Indy 500 car. *How do I know Mom and I can trust Jason? What if he leaves us too?*

"There's Slam, our ferocious watchdog!" called Jason excitedly as we pulled up to the white ranch house. After four days our journey was over at last. The huge dog was all over us the minute Mom opened her door.

"Any intruder on our property would have to move fast to get away from all those dog kisses!" Mom said, laughing, as she watched me giggle and dodge Slam's slurpy tongue. Wiping my face, I knew I'd made my first friend in Montana.

"Where's my cat?" I asked Jason.

"Billy Bob? He usually hangs out on the back porch," my stepdad answered.

Then I saw him—more gorgeous than any cat I'd ever seen in a picture!

"He's all yours—the first of many gifts from your new pops. I promise," Jason added, and I winced.

I hurried toward my feline dream-come-true, intending to sweep my first pet into my arms. But as I approached, Billy Bob transformed himself into a streak of butter that instantly melted into the latticework beneath the porch.

"It's OK," Jason tried to console me. "He doesn't know you well enough to trust you yet, but I promise he will."

Yeah, sure, I thought.

"So when do you want to learn to drive the quad?" Jason asked the next morning.

"The what?" I swallowed a mouthful of pancake. (I had to admit that Mom had married a great cook.)

"The quad. The ATV—all-terrain vehicle," he explained. "After one lesson with me, you'll be a great driver. I promise." This time Jason caught my cold glare.

"What's wrong?" he asked.

"How come you keep saying 'I promise' all the time?"

"Honey," Mom interjected, setting her orange juice down, "what a strange question."

"No, it's not!" I snapped. "Not when you-know-who broke every promise he ever made to me!"

Jason and Mom exchanged startled glances.

"But I'm not you-know-who," Jason said in a patient voice.

"You may not be you-know-who," I spat out in anger that seemed to come out of nowhere, "but don't expect me to believe your stupid promises any more than I could ever believe his!" With that I ran from the kitchen, down the walk toward the barn, and threw myself onto some bales of hay. There I cried about what I'd lost from the past—and all I feared for the future.

When my sobbing stopped, I felt hay poking me. Sitting up, I rubbed my itching arms and thought, *After what I said to Jason, I guess him teaching me to ride the quad is one promise he definitely won't keep!*

Just then Slam bounded up beside me on the hay as Jason called out in the distance, "Whenever you're ready to ride, you can find me unpacking the trailer."

As it turned out, Jason was right. After just one lesson on the quad, I got around pretty well. As the days went by, Slam would race down the dirt road ahead of me, barking and chasing jackrabbits. Billy Bob, on the other hand, would just watch us leave and return. Slowly he became somewhat friendlier, as Jason had me feeding him. Once in a while my pet would even rub up against my jeans or let me dangle a string for him to bat at with his paws.

"Good for you," Jason would say when he saw this. "Billy's learning that you're not going to hurt him. That's what trust is all about." With a wink, he'd playfully add, "I promise."

One morning two weeks after I'd started driving the quad, Slam jumped up behind me and started licking my left ear. Surprised, I hollered for Mom and Jason to come see us take our first slow ride together. From the porch Billy Bob also watched.

Later that week, after doing my chores and feeding Billy Bob, I called, "Let's go for a ride, Slam!" He followed me to the garage and jumped behind the driver's seat. Carefully backing out the ATV, I centered the handlebars and slowly started down the road toward the mailbox. That's when it happened.

Billy Bob, who'd gone to the barn to hunt mice, leaped from a bale of hay and came out toward us, meowing. Squeezing the brakes, I stopped the quad and called, "Billy Bob, what is it?"

He paused about three feet from the quad before approaching more cautiously. "Meow."

"What do you want, Billy Bob?" I asked, thinking the loud engine of the quad would frighten him away.

Instead he continued approaching my left cowboy boot. Then without warning, he jumped straight up into my lap. Settling himself between my knees, he put his front paws up on the handlebars.

I could hardly believe it. I slowly released the brakes and started rolling down the hill, with Slam's long ears flapping the sides of his head and Billy Bob's eyes squinting into the wind.

By the time we returned from our short ride, Billy Bob had turned around with his head pressed into my jacket. His purring was almost as loud as the quad's engine.

When Slam, Billy Bob, and I rounded the last bend into the driveway, Jason looked down at us from the ladder beneath the gutter he was cleaning out. I cut the engine and just sat smiling at him. I couldn't remember when I'd ever felt happier.

"I can hardly believe my eyes!" he exclaimed. "Good job! Looks like Billy Bob passed the trust test with flying colors."

"He sure did!" I yelled back.

"And how about you?" Jason asked. "Have you passed the trust test yet?"

I looked at this new father whom God had brought into my life. Suddenly I realized that this man had kept every promise he'd ever made to me! *Is that what my heavenly Father is like?* I wondered.

Just then I wished Jason were close enough to hug.

"So what about it?" Jason pressed. "Do you trust me yet?"

I swallowed hard and then answered, "Yes, I do. I promise."

27
Jungle Fear
by Helen Lee

We scrambled to our feet as soon as the alarm on Jason's watch started beeping. "Time's up. Let's go," he said, leading the way into the jungle.

For weeks Jason and I had studied the Pathfinders' manual, and today was the day of our big test. Our teacher, Mr. Baum, had met us in front of our school in the Philippines and had driven us through fields of sugarcane to a little clearing.

"Wait here 15 minutes," he had instructed before disappearing into the woods. "Then you can start following the signs."

So here we were, following the signs Mr. Baum had left behind. Hopefully we'd pass the requirements for wilderness tracking.

"There's our first sign," I said, pointing to some rocks in front of us. We hurried to the pile of rocks and squatted down to examine the way they had been placed.

"H'mmm . . . Two rocks here and one rock here," Jason said out loud.

"I know. We're supposed to take a left," I said excitedly. "Look, here's a little trail."

We turned left onto the trail and kept going, slowing down to climb over tree stumps and some fallen logs.

A few minutes later Jason spotted the next sign, a bunch of leaves clustered together in the shape of an arrow. "It says to turn left," Jason said. "We'll be through in no time."

We hurried along deeper and deeper into the jungle. The tall trees blocked most of the sunlight. I pointed to three rocks stacked on top of one another. "That means to keep following the trail."

We walked along, single file, searching for signs, but we didn't see any more. The trail became narrower, and the weeds threatened to take over.

I checked the time on my watch. Fifteen minutes had passed since we had started. "We should be almost done by now," I said.

"Do you think we're still on the right track?" Jason asked, sounding a little worried.

I shrugged. "I don't know. Do you want to turn back?"

"No, let's keep going a little farther," Jason replied.

We kept going but didn't find any more signs. The trail eventually dead-ended at a steep decline. I looked down, but I couldn't see anything because of the branches blocking our view.

"I'll go first and scout it out," Jason volunteered.

I watched him slip and slide toward the bottom. The leaves quickly hid him from view. I stood there, debating if I should follow. It was kind of scary being alone in the jungle. "Jason," I called out.

Suddenly I heard him scrambling back to the top, yelling, "Run!"

I didn't have to be told twice. I turned around and started running as fast as I could. Jason was right behind me. I had no idea what we were running from, but I could only imagine the worst.

Please, Lord, please, I prayed silently.

I carefully dodged low-hanging branches and tried to concentrate on the path. My heart beat faster and faster as my feet pounded along the narrow jungle trail. We ran for a long time, retracing our steps.

"Hey!" Jason and I pointed at the same time to a branch a few yards in front of us.

"We missed a sign," I said, out of breath. "We should have turned here." We turned right and kept running.

"There's another sign," Jason yelled, pointing to some rocks. "Take a left." As soon as we turned, we saw the clearing straight in front of us.

Mr. Baum smiled when he saw us coming. "You made it," he said, giving us hugs. "You had me worried for a while. What happened?"

"We got lost," I said as soon as I caught my breath. "And then we ran into a . . ." I stopped and turned to Jason. "What were we running from?"

"I . . . I . . . I saw something that really scared me," he said. "These big round eyes were staring at me from a tree. I mean . . . I mean, this thing had huge fangs dripping with saliva."

"Do you know what it was?" I asked.

"Well," he hesitated and then started grinning sheepishly. "I've never seen a bigger monkey in my life!"

Mr. Baum and I burst out laughing. "You mean we were running from a monkey?" I exclaimed. "You had me running for my life!"

Jason shrugged. "Sorry. I guess it wasn't that big of a deal," he said with a chuckle.

As we drove home, I thought about things we're afraid of, such as getting up front or looking stupid or losing a game. Sometimes our fears seem monstrous, and we try to run and hide. But if we confront our fears, they may turn out to be no big deal, kind of like the poor monkey in the jungle. I just hope we didn't scare it too badly.

28
Pushing Through to Rawlins
by Elaine Egbert

Thirteen-year-old Clyde buttoned his parka as he leaned forward to peer through the frosty windshield. Outside, snowflakes raced frantically ahead of a fierce wind, whiting out the Wyoming hills and limiting his view to just beyond the car's hood.

Concerned, he glanced at his older brother Roy. "It's a blizzard!" he said. "Can you see well enough to drive?"

Roy didn't answer, but gripped the steering wheel tighter as they inched into the pelting whiteness.

Clyde glanced over his shoulder at Berta and Owen, their older siblings, who dozed fitfully. Would the four of them make it to Rawlins before drifting snow closed the road?

A few weeks earlier Doc Schmidt had told Ma that unless they moved to a milder climate, Sam, their oldest son, would probably die. So in spite of plummeting temperatures, Pa and Ma had quickly loaded the car and left for Idaho, taking Sam and two of their daughters. Clyde and his five other siblings had stayed behind to close down their business and home.

They all knew that winter was a bad time for a family to move, especially in such cold country. But as Pa always said, "When things go wrong, you just hunker down and do what you've gotta do."

Pa and Clyde's brothers ran a car repair garage for their living. After their parents left, Clyde and his siblings packed the garage equipment and the household goods and loaded them onto a boxcar. Two brothers accompanied their belongings to Idaho, where Pa had decided to settle. That left Berta, Owen, Roy, and Clyde to clean and close the house and garage, then drive away from Cowley, Wyoming, for the last time.

Thankful that they were driving Roy's brand-new 1927 Willys Whippet with its good heater, Clyde turned his attention back to the road. He knew that Ma would be praying for them. Though he wasn't certain God listened to prayers, Clyde hoped that He would provide a safe journey. After all, if God would listen to anyone, He'd listen to Ma.

As the afternoon wore on, the snow stopped, yet the wind still whipped the snowflakes already on the ground. Where the fields at the side of the roadway rose higher than the road, drifts would form, leaving white hills across the driving lanes. Soon the drifts became too deep for cars to pass through, so Roy pulled onto the edge of the road.

Berta awakened. "How come we stopped?"

"Drifts. If we try to go through, we could get stranded."

"How much farther to Rawlins?"

Roy sighed. "About 40 miles."

"But if we stay here, we'll freeze!" Berta protested.

Soon Roy turned off the motor to save fuel, and the car quickly cooled. Only a couple hours of daylight remained.

Clyde watched as other cars pulled up behind them. Shivering, he suspected that the temperature had dropped to about −45°F. Spending the night at that temperature would be foolhardy. Though he was the youngest in the car, he knew someone must make a decision that would solve their problem, and there was no time to lose.

"Owen," he announced, "we can't stay here. Let's tromp a track that the tires can follow through the drift. Roy can follow right behind before it drifts over again."

Owen eyed his younger brother. "It's cold enough to freeze your skin instantly. We'd better wait for a snowplow to come through."

But Rawlins was miles away! Already Berta's lips were blue, and it wasn't even dark yet. What was it that Pa always said? "When things go wrong, you just hunker down and do what you've gotta do."

Clyde wrapped his woolen scarf around his face and then pulled up his parka hood. He was not going to just sit back and let nature take its course! "Well, I'm going to try," he said, pushing the door with his shoulder.

The cold hit like an iron fist. Sucking in his breath, Clyde leaned hard into the wind and headed for the drift. Soon Owen joined him. Together they stomped through the drifted snow, packing it in two narrow trails. Clyde heard the crunch of the tires as Roy followed close behind.

Clyde remembered the hot summers in Cowley. He'd worked hard in the garage, cleaning bearings and then cleaning up behind his brothers. But he'd also gone with his pals to swim in the canal or hike up Rattlesnake Canyon. He didn't want to move away and leave his school friends. Cowley was home! He already missed his friends, but down deep he knew he'd miss Sam more if something bad happened to him.

At last Clyde stopped on the far side of the drift and looked back. Behind the Whippet a line of other cars followed in their tracks. When the Whippet pulled up beside them, the boys climbed in and rode to the next drift.

Hour after hour Clyde and Owen tromped through the drifts, until their lungs ached from breathing the frosty air. The cold made their eyes water, then froze the tears on their cheeks. In spite of his warm winter clothes and boots, Clyde's feet numbed, and soon he felt he couldn't take another step. Nevertheless, mile after mile, he and Owen tromped through the drifts. When the sun went down, blackness covered them like a thick blanket. From behind them the Whippet's headlights beamed yellow across the snow.

I wish someone else would tromp drifts for a while! Clyde thought, longing for rest. *But I mustn't quit now.*

Finally, far away, Clyde spied a patch of lights. Was Rawlins still that far? His energy was nearly gone, and the drifts were closer together now. Exhausted, Clyde turned his thoughts to God.

Ma said God listened and helped when people prayed, but Clyde had never thought much about Him, seldom feeling the need for help. Now he wondered if God could provide enough strength to finish his task. But Clyde hadn't bothered going to church or kneeling beside his bed for a long time. Why would God even care about him or what he was trying to do?

"Could You please give me enough energy to tramp the rest of the way into Rawlins?" he finally prayed. "That's asking a lot, but I need help." Clyde couldn't think of anything else to say, so he said "Amen" and then bent to his task. And from somewhere new strength came.

Finally the last drift was conquered, and the tired boys hopped back into the Whippet, which proudly led the procession of cars into Rawlins.

Before going into the hotel, Clyde looked into the inky blackness overhead. Stars twinkled down on him, sending out their glad lights. Somewhere behind those stars, he figured, God lived. And God had heard his prayer!

"Thanks for giving me the energy and persistence to finish the task," Clyde said with a new understanding about God. Soon the family would be together again, and he hoped that everything would go well. But if it didn't? He now knew that he could count on God to help them hunker down and do what they needed to do.

29
Mystery Man on the Shore
by Dawn Clark

Jamie drummed his fingers against the wooden rail on the porch, wishing Carly would hurry. Dad was taking Michael, Carly, and him fishing.

The changing tide was the best time to catch fish. Jamie could just imagine a huge fish dangling from the end of his line. But if Carly didn't hurry, they would miss the incoming tide. On top of that, they'd have to carry all the heavy fishing gear to the water's edge instead of driving there.

"I'm ready," Carly sang out as she waltzed onto the porch and headed toward the car.

Shaking his head, Jamie slid in beside her, while Michael and Dad climbed into the front. Despite his irritation with his younger sister, Jamie was looking forward to wading in the surf and feeling the cool ocean breezes blowing on his face.

Arriving at the beach, Dad drove the car onto the warm, packed sand and parked near the surf. Within minutes they had baited their fishing hooks and cast the lines into the water.

"Keep an eye on the tide, Carly," Dad warned. "Let us know when it starts coming in."

"OK, Dad," Carly replied.

Jamie watched Carly cast her line from near the water's edge. *She's pretty good at fishing—for a girl,* he thought.

Picking up his own rod, Jamie headed into the deeper water, stopping when it reached his knees. The waves were higher than usual today and the undercurrents stronger. Jamie knew he would have to be careful.

There must be a storm brewing somewhere off the coast, Jamie thought as he prepared to cast his line, struggling to keep his balance in the pounding surf. Wave after wave surged over his knees, some climbing high on his thighs. The water felt wonderful, though, after spending the long, hot morning working in the garden.

Despite its beauty, Jamie knew how treacherous the ocean could be. It could turn on him in an instant, pulling him out to sea.

Once his line was in the water, Jamie began to relax and enjoy the peaceful setting, forgetting all about the rising tide. As he reeled in his line and recast it, he couldn't imagine a more perfect way to spend an afternoon.

All of a sudden an unusually large wave rose from the ocean and struck Jamie on the chest, knocking him off his feet. Jamie's arms flailed helplessly as he was pulled under the water and rolled along the sea floor. Still clutching the fishing rod, he struggled to the surface and regained his footing.

Glancing at the shore to get his bearings, Jamie drew up short, his heart pounding with fear. The same wave that had knocked him over had reached the car. The tide was coming in, and it was coming in fast.

"Dad," Jamie screamed as he plowed through the water toward shore, "look at the car!"

The rising tide lapped around the wheels, washing the sand out from under the tires and causing them to sink deeper into the wet sand.

Dropping his fishing rod, Jamie reached the car at the same time Dad, Michael, and Carly did. They had to get the car out—there was no money to buy a new one! Jamie stood at the rear of the car with Dad on one side and Carly and Michael on the other.

"Let's all push together," Dad yelled.

Jamie began pushing, muscles quivering and shaking. Sweat gathered on his forehead, and his breathing became ragged as he struggled against the suction of the gripping sand.

Stopping to catch his breath, Jamie looked up and down the beach. There was not another person in sight for as far as he could see in either direction—no one else who could help them push the car out of the rising sea.

The water was halfway up the wheels now as the tide continued to rise.

"Pray, kids," Dad commanded. "Pray that God will give us the strength to get the car out."

Jamie sent prayer after prayer to heaven, begging God to help the family save their car from the ocean's grip.

Suddenly a stranger stood at Dad's side and began pushing with everyone else. Jamie stared at him in confusion, wondering where he had come from. There had been no one else on the beach a few seconds earlier. With a shrug of his shoulders he dismissed his questions and began pushing again.

He felt the car shift. Excitement leaped through him as he redoubled his efforts. He could hear the grunts and groans of those around him.

The car moved again. There was a sucking noise as the sand reluctantly released its grip on the wheels, allowing the car to break free. With one final heave the car rolled out of the water and onto firmer ground.

Resting his hands on his knees, Jamie drew great, gulping breaths of air into his lungs. He felt a smile growing on his face as he watched his family high-fiving one another and celebrating their victory over the sea. Jamie's dad walked up to him and clapped a hand on his shoulder.

"Good job, son," he said, pulling him into a hug.

With Dad's hand still resting across Jamie's shoulder, the two turned to thank the mysterious stranger for his help in pushing the car out of the surging waters. No one was there. Perplexed, the family stood on the sand looking around in all directions. The man could not be seen anywhere.

How could someone vanish into thin air? Jamie wondered. But that seemed to be exactly what had happened. No one else was on the beach except for their family and a group of seagulls flying overhead.

Then Jamie noticed something very unusual. "Hey, Dad," he called. "Look at the sand."

Dad studied the sand, a puzzled expression on his face. "How is that possible?" Dad whispered. "There are no footprints in the sand where the stranger was standing."

"No, Dad, there aren't," Jamie answered. "Look up and down the beach, too—no footprints there, either." Jamie stood with his dad, a look of wonder on his face.

"It was an angel," Jamie said, slowly smiling. "God sent us our very own personal angel to help us when no one else was around."

"I believe you're right, Jamie," Dad answered, a grin tugging at the corners of his mouth. "God did answer our prayers for help."

"Let's thank Him," Jamie said.

The family held hands and knelt in the sand. With hearts full of praise they thanked God for sending an angel in their moment of distress.

30
Janna's Offering
by Elfriede Volk

Janna was pale and skinny, with pigtails hanging halfway down her back. Her family were refugees from some country or other. They lived in the cabin just down from us, without running water, without electricity, without heat. Her father worked as a day laborer at a logging camp.

Every morning and evening Janna's father took care of the cow and few chickens someone had given them. He mowed hay by hand to have something to feed the cow in the winter. But he couldn't make enough hay before the snow came, so he brought home a cartful of food scraps from the camp kitchen each day.

I suspected that the family ate from those scraps too. Their clothes certainly were something I would have thrown away. Janna, at 10, almost 11, wore a woman's dress that came down to her ankles and looked like a tent. The sad thing is that she didn't realize how ridiculous she looked.

Mom didn't seem to notice either. She often invited Janna over, and the girl invariably stayed for dinner. Once we had a trifle with bananas for dessert. Janna ate as if she had never tasted bananas before.

"Maybe she hasn't," Mom said when I commented to her about it. "In many countries people don't have the things we take for granted."

"But why do you always have to give them things? Like the chairs you gave them last week. Shouldn't they work and earn money to buy things for themselves?"

"Yes, if they can. But Janna and her family don't know English, so it's hard for her father to get a decent job. And even if he had the money, it still would be difficult for him to buy things, because he can't understand the salespeople and they can't understand him. Besides, how would he get chairs home? He has no transportation, and town is too far away to carry them."

The next day Mom found something else she could give—English lessons to Janna. Janna was eager to learn, and soon even I could understand her. Mom also invited the family to come to church with us and promised that she would pick them up.

When Janna came to church, she was the center of attention. At first I didn't want to be seen with her, but then I realized that I had to be with her to get my share of the attention. Rather than making fun of me, people actually told me how nice I was, making friends with this poor girl. I felt pleased and guilty at the same time.

Sabbath school fascinated Janna. Afterward, when we were home again, she wanted to act out a Bible story.

Snow was another thing Janna had never seen before, at least not as much as we got that year. She couldn't seem to get enough of it, piling it up and making snow forts and castles. I wondered if she didn't get cold without boots, without mittens, and with only a threadbare coat that didn't fit properly. Her stockings, held up with rubber bands, sometimes slipped down, and I could see her bright-red skin underneath.

"I sort of wish we could do something for Janna," I said when I came home one day. "Something nice."

"Well, we could invite the family for Christmas dinner . . ." Mom suggested.

"Too late. The Reiths already invited them."

"When is her birthday?"

"I don't know, but I'll ask her."

It turned out that she couldn't have been born at a worse time. "Right between Christmas and New Year's," I told Mom. "December 30."

"Will she have a party?"

I snorted. "How can you have a party when you don't even have enough to eat or to wear?"

"Then let's give her one," Mom said. "A surprise birthday party, and we'll invite all the people from church."

Christmas came first. I noticed that there were no decorations at Janna's house. I wasn't surprised.

"What do you do for Christmas?" I asked her.

"We don't celebrate Christmas," she said. "My father says it's a pagan holiday."

"Don't you get any presents?"

"No."

I told Mom. She must have told others at church, because the Sabbath before Christmas one man gave Janna a dollar. She held it as if it was a treasure and kept looking at it, as if unable to believe that it really was hers.

We took up the Thirteenth Sabbath Offering that day. The Sabbath school superintendent said it would be used to build an orphanage in Korea. She said that many children sleep on the streets and rummage through garbage cans to find something to eat. I felt sick, but Janna seemed to be jumping up and down with excitement.

"I have a dollar!" she said excitedly. "Can I give it to help the orphans?"

"No!" said the man who had given it to her. "That money is for you to spend on yourself."

"But I don't need anything," Janna protested, "and these children do. I know what it's like to live through a war. I know what it's like to sleep on the cold ground. I know what it's like to be hungry. Here we have so much. I want to give this money to help these children."

As Janna spoke, I noticed several people wiping their eyes. The offering collected that day was the largest ever. But the giving wasn't over. After church several people handed Janna some money or slipped it into her pocket. Each time she went to the church treasurer and turned it in for the offering.

We stayed in town until after sundown. Then Mom took Janna and me to the dollar store.

"Janna," she said, "I want you to help me find some presents for a father and a mother. They need to be something special, because the people are special."

Janna looked at many things, then chose a large mug for the father and some thick pot holders for the mother.

"These are for you to give to your father and mother," Mom said when she had paid for them. "I'll give you some wrapping paper when we get home so that you can wrap them up."

Janna's delight was contagious. After she had gone home, I looked at my doll collection and picked out Clementine. With her curly blond hair and blue dress, she was my favorite.

"Mom," I said, "could I give Clementine to Janna for her birthday?"

Mom hugged me. "I'm proud of you," she said, "for giving your best."

Janna's birthday party was a huge success. Everyone from church was there, and everyone brought gifts for Janna. She ended up with a whole new wardrobe and writing paper and perfume and soaps. And after dinner

Dad hitched up our horse to our sleigh and we went riding through the winter wonderland, singing for joy. It was the kind of joy I had learned about from Janna—the joy of giving.